The
Higginbothams

Vivian Nichols
6-28-2024

Vivian Higginbotham Nichols

Acknowlegements

I want to express my appreciation and thanks to some of my family and friends for their assistance in information they had about the family and from their own personal recollections. Their bits of information helped in my efforts to construct this story.

- Thanks especially goes to my mother, Edna Higginbotham, for always being there for me, not only throughout my life but for this project. She was instrumental in allowing me access to resources, letters, photos, etc. She also answered numerous questions I had and gave me the moral support I needed.
- Without my dad's previous 8 year-long work on his book about his brothers' experiences during WWII, I would not have had those resources. He also provided me so many anecdotes about his family over the years until his death in 2011. He was definitely the family historian.
- Also, I want to thank my sister Linda May. She has always assisted me in geneaology questions and with photos.
- My cousin Cherilyn Wackerly spent time on the phone recalling memories she had from her perspective and memories. She is Mildred's daughter.
- My appreciation also goes to a close family friend, James Edwards, who grew up as a childhood friend to my dad. James spent an hour on the phone recalling events from their childhood together. He later became related through marriage. (His sister Lucille married my Dad's brother, Murphy. Lucille was my closest aunt growing up, and my sister Linda and I spent lots of time with her and her family on camping trips to Florida, Colorado, and Galveston during our formative teen years. She was like a second mother to me and always treated me like one of her own. In addition to my own mother, I will always be thankful for her example of what a Christian woman should look like.)
- I also wish to express my appreciation to my husband Gary who has supported me throughout this extensive process.

Last but not least, I even want to include an appreciation to my seven year-old grandson, "Little John Man." While baby-sitting him and his siblings

3

for a few days, I showed him the first chapter I had completed to this story, along with the photos. As I was explaining the time period of some of them, he brought it to my attention that they lived through the worst pandemic in history during 1918-1919. I thought, "Wow! I had not even thought about that!" From his own personal experience with the current pandemic, he could relate to that for them. Impressive for a seven year-old!

This book is dedicated to the memory of my paternal grandparents and their families. If it were not for Grandma's journal writings and her saving of all the photos, letters, and news articles, my dad Maurice "Scooter" would not have been able to put together and write a book about his brothers' war experiences for the family. Using all of these resources, along with the aforementioned individuals, and my own memories and research, I was able to compose this story. I only hope it does justice to their lives.

Vivian Higginbotham Nichols

Joseph "Mid" & Ida Higginbotham holding Marvin
1914

The Higginbothams

I realize the "Greatest Generation" refers to those who were coming of age during the Great Depression and who lived through WWII, but I believe my grandparents who preceded them also earned that title, at least in my family. They were the ones, who after all, bore the responsibilities of struggling through the Great Depression to raise that generation, only to see four of their five sons march off to war. The only reason my dad did not march off alongside his brothers was due to his young age of seven during the attack on Pearl Harbor. His only surviving sister, Mildred, was 24 years old and already married and out of the house. That left Grandma and Grandpa Higginbotham to keep the home fires burning for the rest of the family while trying to raise my dad, Maurice "Scooter."

After my grandmother Ida Williams survived her horrifying childhood in the mountains of Arkansas during the late nineteenth century, (which was detailed in my previous book, *Whisper Mountain*) she wanted to leave her past behind, so she decided to move to Houston, Texas, about 80 miles west of her sister Emma who was living in Guffey. It was 1912 and Ida was just 21 years of age and earnestly longing to make a fresh start with a new identity. What she did not realize at that time was her emotional scars would haunt her for the rest of her life.

Ida was fortunate enough to land a job at one of the local boarding houses. Mrs. Warren and Mrs. Munger were the two ladies she worked for, and she loved them because they treated her so kindly. This provided her with living expenses plus a place to stay without paying rent. However, it was terribly exhausting work. Besides the eleven rooms that she had to keep clean, there were the porches and walkways that had to be swept. That was the easy part. She also had to wash the laundry, iron the linens, do the cooking, and wash the dishes before retiring for the night.

Washing laundry was not that simple in those days. She had to build a fire outside and bring water to a boil in a huge cast iron pot before inserting the towels and linens. Then she would stir in lye soap with the laundry until they were clean before taking them out and putting them into clean water to rinse. That was before wringing them out and hanging them out to dry. But it gave her a sense of pride and fulfillment in her abilities to provide for herself, so she worked happily at her tasks, never complaining.

Ida at Mrs. Warren & Mrs. Munger's Boarding House in
Houston 1912

Eventually, Ida felt she just had to go visit Nan who was
living in Louisiana. She and Nan had been inseparable during
their childhood after all they had been through together, and
she just could not bear not being able to see her. Although
they had corresponded through letters, it just was not the
same. The past few years without her were just too much, so
she quit her job in Houston and headed to DeRidder.

When Ida arrived at Nan's house, her sister was
overjoyed. They enjoyed a heartfelt visit and caught up on
what had been happening since they had seen each other last.
There was so much to talk over, and they reminisced about
their tumultuous childhood. It had forever changed their
perspectives on life, and they never wanted to feel vulnerable
like that again, so they vowed to always have one another's
back during times of trouble.

After several days had passed Nan gave her a tour around town. Ida loved the small town atmosphere and the friendly people, especially those she met while attending the local Hopewell Baptist Church several miles east of town. That is where Grandma met my grandfather, Joseph Middleton "Mid" Higginbotham. It did not take long before they both realized they were meant for each other. During a ceremony in that sanctuary, they were both united in matrimony on February 16, 1913. She was 22 and Mid was 23, and they were forever joined in heart and spirit. Their love and devotion to one another was inspirational, but their later trials would dig up old wounds for Ida. There was her insecurity about not being loved as a child that would raise its ugly head now and then.

Mid's father, George Washington Higginbotham, had previously been the preacher at the Hopewell Baptist Church until his death. His father had suffered with a chronic ulcer on his right leg since childhood. It eventually turned into gangrene. During the fall of 1903, Dr. Singleton from Sugartown arrived in his horse-drawn buggy in order to amputate his leg. There was no anesthesia at the time, so they got him drunk with whiskey. Mid's mother, Anna Eliza Barrow Higginbotham, was by her husband's side.

Some of the children from the family were curious and wanted to watch, but the doctor sent them away and told them they needed to show reverence at what had to be done, so they watched from a distance. The poor fellow could be heard screaming throughout the procedure. To show respect for the amputated limb, they conducted a burial for it with the children present.

George complained for a while that it felt like ants were biting his leg. Finally, they dug up his leg and found ants all over it, so they rewrapped it and fixed it so ants could not get to it and reburied it. He stopped complaining about the ant bites.

A land grant of 170.21 acres had previously been issued to George on the 10th of October, 1896. It was signed by President Grover Cleveland. The property was located near the intersection of Hopewell Church Road on Hwy 1147. He had deeded some of the land to Mid so he could build his own house.

Mid had built a nice log house and a barn on the property about a quarter-mile past Welbourn Crossing opposite Bundick's Creek from the Hopewell Baptist Church. That is where the new bride and groom would live.

The first thing the newlyweds did was to purchase a cast iron wash pot in order to do their laundry over a fire and a crock bowl in order to make their biscuits. They lived and worked on Mid's farm for the next seven years. It was the first time Ida considered herself the owner of any real property, and she was sure thankful Mid already owned his own farm, along with a horse and buggy. Other than walking, this was their only mode of transportation.

Located about 14 miles east of DeRidder, the farm was surrounded by thick woods, along with the wild animals and snakes known about the area. Humidity and heat were usually a huge factor during summer months due to its location near the swamp lands and the Gulf of Mexico about 70 miles to the south. The humid air hung so heavily about them, it seemed you could slice it with a knife. Mosquitoes and other insects were relentless at times and caused much concern and misery for man and beast.

Mid also worked in the timber industry for The Hudson River Lumber Company which cut, dried, and shipped millions of board feet of lumber each year, thanks to the completion of the Gulf, Colorado and Santa Fe Railroad east-west line that ran from Kirbyville, Texas through DeRidder and on to Oakdale. These kinds of work were extremely exhausting but also fulfilling for the young couple; they felt like they were building a happy, successful life together.

As often as they were able, they attended the sanctuary where they had married. Ida learned to love these people and appreciate their words of encouragement. They seemed like an extension of family who genuinely cared for her and Mid.

Thankfully, Mid also had plenty of family nearby. Besides his five older sisters, Roxyann, Harriet, Martha, Margaret, and Mary, he had two brothers, Frank and Simon who always offered help when needed. Mid was the youngest of his clan, but his siblings were always glad to assist when needed. He trusted and appreciated their maturity and experiences. They in turn appreciated his help at times.

One day Mid stopped by for a visit at his sister Margaret's farm and realized that his little niece Thedda was out in the field helping her father pick cotton while she was running a fever and sick. She told him her jaws hurt, so he realized she had the mumps. He told her to go to the house and go to bed, that he would finish picking her cotton. Not only was he mild-mannered, he was just a very thoughtful and kind man. Although Mid exhibited many acts of selflessness throughout the years, that one act of kindness remained with Thedda the remainder of her life and was the reason she always claimed Mid was her favorite uncle.

2

It was not long before Ida became pregnant. Knowing they would soon be new parents was very exhilarating for the young couple, so they made preparations and worked earnestly at them. Nan and her family also shared in the excitement, so they helped prepare for the upcoming event. The two sisters worked passionately together sewing baby clothes and stitching a quilt for the occasion. Finally, Ida would have a child of her own on which to shower her love and blessings and hopefully erase some of the wounds from her childhood. She was bound and determined to let her child know just how important he or she was to her and how much she loved him or her.

On November 1, 1913 their first child and infant daughter Ethel was born but passed away on the same day. This devastated the new parents and took the wind out of their sails for quite some time. Once again Ida felt lost and alone. When she was in her quiet and pensive moods, she developed a nervous habit of plaiting her hair. Mid tried his best to console her, but he was somewhat helpless in that endeavor, but he encouraged her every step of the way. Between working the farm and cutting logs for the local sawmill, he felt like his efforts were limited, but he pressed dutifully forward, determined to be the best husband he could be. His soft-spoken mannerisms and his musical talents playing the fiddle and harmonica were soothing to her. Holding her tightly and speaking softly into her ear helped most in reassuring her.

Ida worked hard at staying busy because it was the only way she could deal with her great loss, especially when Mid was away working in the fields or at the timber mill. At times she would join him in the garden and help out. Raising the prettiest gardens and always having plenty of corn, potatoes, beans, cantaloupes, and watermelons made her appreciate him all the more. Not only was her sweetheart a sexy man, he was everything she had hoped for. Aside from her dad who had been murdered when she was only a year old, Mid was the first man who she fully trusted. Without him she would truly be lost.

It was only three months before Ida became pregnant again; this lifted her spirits greatly but at the same time caused her great concern. What if she lost this child, too? She did not feel she could handle losing another baby. Although Nan and Mid tried to allay her fears, Ida knew there was always that possibility, so it was hard for her to shake that feeling. Many prayers were sent up for this infant to be healthy. The young couple relied on their *faith and* held *hope* in their hearts. Ida was also grateful for the baby clothes and quilt she and her sister had happily stitched together for Ethel. In those days infant clothes were basically made the same. There were no boy or girl clothes because they were all little gowns for either sex.

On November 17, 1914, Marvin Douglas was born, and his parents were elated because he seemed to be a picture of health. Mid and Ida worked extra hard to ensure all of his needs were met and all of his clothes were kept washed and dried. Of course, the diapers were the most challenging job of all. They also had no idea how often his little gowns had to be washed and dried due to his spitting up all over them.

Like all babies, Marvin was no exception to having stomach aches or running fever occasionally. There were times his parents were beside themselves with worry. Parenting was a lot more challenging than the young couple had anticipated, but they struggled through with flying colors. If they could not figure out his problem, they would simply do their best to console him. Ida learned the trick of giving him a "sugar tit," a little butter and sugar mixed together and wrapped in a clean cloth for him to suck on. Pacifiers were non-existent then, at least in the woods of Louisiana.

The young and small family of three struggled like most families getting established and thriving, but it was certainly no small task. Since Mid did not want to leave a horse around the mill all day to worry about and take care of, he would catch a ride with Frank the few miles to work and then back home afterwards. Besides, he wanted to leave his wagon for Ida and Marvin in case of an emergency. Mid had enough hard physical labor cutting timber all day, but he still had to tend his gardens during the spring and summer months. Often he would slip away to hunt small game so there would be meat to go along with their crops. Many times he came home with squirrel or rabbits.

At certain times of the year, he would also hunt larger game such as deer or wild hogs. The larger animals required a lot more time to process, so he usually waited until cooler weather when he was not working his garden. Frank and Simon would help Mid butcher the larger animals. When one of the brothers killed a deer or hog, they would usually join forces to process them. Families relied on each other often and did not hesitate to help.

Ida also had her hands full tending to Marvin, cooking her famous biscuits, cleaning the house, and washing the laundry. Every morning began early for her. First she had to build a fire in the cook stove before mixing her biscuit dough and preparing them for the pan and placing them in the oven. While they baked she fried pork or whatever meat was on hand and fried or scrambled the eggs.

After breakfast was finished she had to heat water for the dishes, wash them and put them away before preparing for the midday meal. It seemed she hardly left the kitchen unless it was to take care of Marvin, and there was no electricity in the farm house to run lights or fans. The only way she could cope was to raise the window. This provided a small bit of sunlight and fresh air. If she were lucky she might occasionally feel a breeze.

When Marvin was old enough to start toddling around, Mid and Ida decided to barter for more chickens and buy a cow so they would always have enough fresh eggs and milk. This added more responsibilities because the cow had to be fed and milked, and the chickens had to be fed and the eggs had to be gathered, but they sure enjoyed the fruits of their labor.

Ida skimmed the cream and churned it into butter. Adding the correct amount of salt was important to enhance its natural flavor, but she eventually perfected her craft. Because she had already fine-tuned her biscuit recipe, the butter made them irresistible! Mid and Marvin could not seem to get enough of them, and this was even before the annual syrup mill operation was held and they could add ribbon cane syrup to their feast.

Louisiana was known for its sugar cane, and every November there would be a local syrup mill running its operation and selling its products. Folks would come from miles around to watch the spectacle and purchase enough syrup to last until the next year's event.

A mule was harnessed to a machine that pulled the long cane stalks through, squeezing the juice into a long pipe that funneled it down into a large open vat. A man fed the long stalks through the machine and continued to encourage the animal to keep walking in circles. The vat was perched above a fire where the juice could be cooked down into syrup. As the mule walked in a never-ending circle, the man would continually add new sugar cane stalks to the device so the juice could continue to be extracted. Another man holding a very long paddle would stir the syrup as needed. The enticing aroma excited the crowds who had gathered to watch.

This event not only provided neighbors with a much-loved product, but it also provided them with an important social event. People would spend hours visiting and catching up on the local comings and goings and the latest news. The children would run around and play. Sometimes folks would bring their instruments and sit around and play music and sing. Mid enjoyed playing his fiddle and harmonica on occasions. It was a festive time that everyone looked forward to. It was certainly a respite from the hard, back-breaking work that took place most of the year. Their *faith and hope* for the future gave them the motivation to keep moving forward, and this event certainly helped renew their spirits.

3

It would only be a couple of years before Ida realized she was with child again, and the family began making preparations for another addition to their small family; however, it was only two months into her pregnancy that the couple began hearing reports about German submarines attacking and sinking some of the United States merchant and passenger ships, causing the deaths of many U. S. seamen and citizens. On April 6, 1917, Mid came in from work and announced, "The United States just declared war on Germany!"

Of course, Marvin was too young to understand what the excitement and extra activity were all about. Suddenly, Mid and his colleagues had to work overtime at The Hudson River Timber Company, cutting extra lumber for the military efforts. This only added stress on the family, especially on Ida. Here she was expecting another child to care for, and Mid was away more than usual. Worry seemed to occupy her mind. When she had a moment to sit and rest, she would plait her hair and pray.

After Mid would come in from working long, hard hours at the mill, he would do his best to encourage her and ease her mind, but his facade was transparent. He, too, was concerned about the war and its eventual outcome, not only for the country but for his young family. They were both thankful for their brothers and sisters who lived nearby. It was times like this where they definitely needed one another's moral support, and it was times like this they relied on their *faith* in God *and hope* that things would end well for everyone.

Five months into the war Mildred Opal made her appearance into the world. It was September 12th, two months before Marvin's third birthday. He was spell-bound by this tiny infant and eventually learned to become very protective of her. Mid and Ida fell in love with this little girl. She reminded them so much of Ethel. Their life seemed complete with both a son and a daughter. Aside from peace on earth, what more could they ask for?

As war efforts exploded, the Hudson River Timber Company had so many military orders to fill they had to hire enough workers to run two 10-hour shifts, one by day and one by night. Families flooded to the area when they heard about the job opportunities. This caused a sudden growth to the population of DeRidder. Even though electricity had already been brought into town, it was becoming more available to local businesses as they expanded their operations.

With the influx of people came more war news from those who had connections to those news sources. This caused a general anxiety that permeated throughout the community, but it also energized folks to work harder in their efforts to support the United States' war efforts. They were united in spirit and purpose. Everyone seemed to be in tune to their neighbors, and everyone was anxious to help their fellow man when needed.

One cool morning the following March, Ida was up early as usual tending to 6 month-old Mildred and trying to get breakfast prepared for Mid before he had to leave for work. Thankfully, Marvin was still sleeping. Suddenly, she became very nauseated and weak. Alarmed, Mid helped her to a chair. "What's the matter, Sweetheart?"

"I'm not sure. It just hit me all of a sudden."

Mid brought her a glass of cool water and she sipped it slowly.

"I feel like I need a bite of something."

Mid fetched a piece of bread and handed it to her.

"Thank you." She nibbled on the bread slowly and washed it down with some water. "I feel a little better now."

"Try to take it easy today. I'll hurry home after work and check on you."

"Thank you, Hon. I think I'll be fine now."

Mid finished preparing breakfast for the family before heading out for work. He was hoping Ida was not coming down sick, and he was wondering if he would be able to take off from work if she were too sick to take care of herself and the children. It seemed all hands had to be on deck at the mill since the war had started. His thoughts were with her throughout the day.

As Ida went about the day tending to the baby and little Marvin and wondering what was going on inside her, she had an epiphany. She was pregnant again! The rest of her day was filled with conflicting emotions. *What are we going to do? What will Mid say? How can I tend to another baby? Mildred's not a year old, yet!* On the other hand, *God is blessing us with another child! Will it be a boy or girl? I can't wait to tell Nan!*

Periodically throughout the day, Ida would well up in tears. She honestly did not know how to feel. From the news she was hearing daily, the whole world seemed to be at war; however, down here in DeRidder, Louisiana, everyone seemed to get along just fine. While she plaited her hair, she convinced herself that was all that mattered.

After worrying all day about Ida, Mid arrived home dirty and tired but anxious to know how she was feeling. Attempting to read her body language was difficult because she was visibly emotional. *What is she about to tell me? Is it bad news?* He grabbed her close and asked what was wrong. When she explained that she was sure she was pregnant again, Mid gave an audible sigh of relief. "That's wonderful! After I prayed for you today, I felt like everything would be alright. I'm so thankful you're not sick!"

Tears streamed down Ida's cheeks. She was so relieved that her sweetheart was so understanding and kind. Secretly, she had worried he would be upset due to having to provide for another mouth to feed, but she also understood she would have an added responsibility. It was a good thing they could work through these challenges together.

Due to the time of year, Mid had begun preparing his garden for the spring and summer. Although he worked extremely hard hours at the mill every day, he rode the few miles home and worked his garden until nearly dark, without ever complaining.

Ida also worked hard all day, cooking, cleaning, caring for the children, and she would also help Mid in the garden when he was home. She would spread a quilt on the ground for Mildred and place Marvin in the dirt to play while she worked. It just made her happy to be near her man, and it did not seem she had enough time with him.

This work schedule continued through the hot, unbearable summer months. They would take frequent water breaks under the shade trees to cool off. Neither of them complained. They knew what had to be done, and they just did it. However, Ida was beginning to show and slow down a bit.

By the time September arrived and temperatures and humidity began moderating to more favorable levels, work outside seemed more enjoyable. Most of the garden had already been harvested, canned, and stored away. However, the animals still had to be cared for, and Mid had begun chopping wood for winter.

Saturdays were usually reserved for doing the laundry. Because it took a few hours, this was a joint effort. Mid would build the fire and get the wash pot filled with water while Ida gathered the laundry and lye soap. Boiling and stirring the clothes with a big wooden paddle helped to get them clean. Then the dirty water had to be emptied and clean rinse water added. Again, Ida would stir the clothes with the paddle until she knew they were clean. Each piece of laundry had to be squeezed and hung out to dry. Mid did as much as he could and realized she did not have long until the new baby would be born.

About midway through September, they began hearing reports about a flu outbreak in the Port of New Orleans, a little over two hundred miles to the southeast of them. It wasn't long before the reports were becoming more ominous.

4

An oil tanker had arrived with five crewmembers ill with bad cases of influenza. In fact, one had already died enroute. These patients were removed from the ship and placed into what was considered a safe location. Within a few short days, things had gotten badly out of hand, and the illness was spreading like wildfire. This was very unsettling news for Mid and Ida, especially since she was due to deliver her new baby soon. And there were Marvin and Mildred to worry about coming down sick. Ida was beside herself. She plaited her hair more than usual.

Merrion Gailion was born on November 17, 1918 into a world that seemed to be in upheaval. At least World War I had ended a few days prior on November 11th, but with the increasing pandemic at hand, things had not had time to settle down at all. In fact, the war at home had just begun.

Mid and Ida soon began hearing reports about New Orleans shutting down public events and even the schools because the death rate was astronomically high, and there was no known remedy for the illness at the time. Between October 1918 and April 1919 there were 54,089 reported cases in New Orleans alone, with 3,489 deaths – a fatality rate of 6.5%. That did not include all the cases outside the city or in the surrounding towns like DeRidder, and the reporting in those days lacked accuracy because there were so many unreported cases.

Even though many of the cases of pneumonia were direct results of the flu, each was counted as a separate illness, so deaths from pneumonia were not included in those statistics. Worldwide cases were estimated at over 500 million with 50 million deaths, an estimated 10% fatality rate. In other words, 10 people out of every 100 presumably died from it.

At least with the war over, the lumber orders dwindled enough to cut back at the mill. Folks were glad to distance themselves at first from their neighbors in order to lessen their chances of becoming infected with the flu. This provided neighbors a chance to focus on their own needs for the following months until the threat seemed to abate.

With three small children on the farm now, Mid and Ida stayed extremely busy. Mid hunted and processed their meat and also chopped and stacked the wood for winter. Ida was busy with three little ones and had very little time to catch a break. One day while Mid was gone off hunting and Ida was working in the yard and tending to animals, Marvin and Mildred led Merrion "Sim" (He had acquired the nickname from calling persimmons "sims.") up on a hill to "plant a garden." The children realized there were too many weeds, so they decided to burn it off. Their fire quickly spread to one of the neighbor's. They made a dash to their mother.

Later when they realized the neighbor's barn had been destroyed and it had been reported to lawmen, the children were scared to death. Then they saw the deputy approaching their house. Thinking they were going straight to jail, the children hid under the bed and begged their mother to tell the lawmen that she did not have any children.

Another time Ida decided to take Marvin, Mildred, and Sim for a walk in the woods to harvest hickory nuts. Suddenly, a black panther let out a blood-curdling scream.

Ida rushed the children back home and inside, slamming the door behind them. Later that night the panther showed up on their front porch.

Besides these incidents, they felt relatively safe at home on the farm, at least from the virus. That was until Mid developed a persistent cough. It was very troubling and worrisome, especially during the pandemic. *What if he were coming down with the flu? If he does, will the children and Ida catch it? If they did, would any of them die?* His cough seemed to linger for weeks. They tried every home remedy they could imagine, including suggestions from their families. Nothing seemed to stop his coughing.

In spite of his cough, Mid continued to work around the farm. What else could he do? Ida tried her best to watch after him and doctor him with different remedies, but his coughing continued. Months passed and it was taking a toll on the couple. Ida plaited her hair and prayed often. Sensing her anxiety, Mid offered words of encouragement to her. His *faith and hope* were evident, even in times of great trial. He was the strongest man she had ever known.

Finally, Ida convinced Mid that he needed to see a doctor in town. He was diagnosed with tuberculosis. That was like a death sentence then. There was no cure. You just had to live with it and prolong life as long as possible. Ida and Mid's whole family were heartbroken. Ida cried incessantly, but she tried to hide her grief from her sweetheart and her children. She could not imagine what he was going through.

Since the doctor had advised Mid to move to a drier climate like Arizona or Colorado, they decided on Colorado.

They both preferred the mountains over the desert, but they would have to go where he could find work.

Leaving family and friends behind would be gut-wrenching. They felt they had no option; they were forced to leave their beloved farm and all their possessions to the family. It would have been difficult enough on the whole family if they had just wanted to move to a different area, but to have them forced out, not knowing if they would ever see them again was devastating.

Thedda remembered seeing them stop by their farm on the way to the train station. It was early 1920. Mid, Ida, and the three children were riding in their horse-drawn wagon, and everyone was really worried and upset. Nobody wanted them to leave, but they believed what the doctor had said and accepted it without question. They only hoped the drier climate would prolong his life.

After Mid, Ida, and their children stopped by the other family farms to say their goodbyes, they were off to the train station. So many tears flowed that day. Even though Marvin knew they were moving, he was too young to fully understand the implications about his father's disease. He was only five years old. Mildred was two, and Sim was 16 months old. They had no idea what lay ahead for them. It was Mid and Ida's indomitable *faith and hope* that drove them forward.

Mid & Ida holding Sim; Mildred, Marvin 1919

5

When they arrived at the train station in DeRidder, they purchased a one-way ticket for the family to LaJunta, Colorado. The long train ride took them west into the piney woods of East Texas, much like they were accustomed to seeing around DeRidder. The connecting route then turned them north through Texas and into Oklahoma and then Kansas, where the landscape was sparse of trees. This is where they transferred to a westbound train on into Colorado.

It was March 10, 1920 when Mid was blessed by landing a job with the Atchison Topeka and Santa Fe Railroad Company. The company had begun operations in the community back in December 1875, but it wasn't until May 15, 1881 that LaJunta was incorporated. The name was Spanish for "the junction" because the town was located where the northwest bound Oregon Trail split off from the southwest bound Santa Fe Trail. The clean small town also sat along the south bank of the Arkansas River.

They rented a house at 502 E. Fifth Street, just a few blocks from the train station and a few blocks from the First Baptist Church. Of course, Mid could easily walk to work every day, and the whole family could walk to church services on Sundays. In fact, they were perfectly located in town with easy access to whatever needs that might arise. What a relief to the couple! Although Ida had grown up in the mountains of Arkansas, this place was oddly strange to anything Mid had been accustomed. There were views of snow-covered mountains, and the air was noticeably drier. He could not imagine any place more beautiful!

Soon after being hired, he was informed he needed to join the O. R. E., a local Railroad Employees Union. A receipt dated March 10, 1920 for his certificate fee of $1 and his monthly union due fees of $4.30 were later found by his family. There were also receipts found for a 50 cent water bill and a $6 rent payment for a quarter of the month. Apparently, they paid rent on a weekly basis.

Living in LaJunta was far different from living in the humid, pest-laden woods of Louisiana. The air felt crisp, and the family was not burdened with insects and heat. Even when temperatures were the highest during summer months, they could sit under the shade of a tree and thoroughly enjoy the mountain breezes. Mid's cough even improved. The family seemed to be thriving and enjoying the town and its people. Though they really missed their families, this seemed like paradise.

With Marvin enrolled in school, Ida was able to focus her time on tending to Mildred and Sim and on all the cooking and cleaning that needed to be done. This included hauling buckets of water and building fires in the cook stove before she could do either. In many ways life was not much different here than in the woods of Louisiana, except for the higher altitude and the thinner air.

They had only lived there four months when Ida became pregnant again. Since there was no family nearby, she relied on members of her church to help her out when necessary; they were more than happy to assist. Whether it was watching the children for a short time or just giving moral support, they were willing to do so. Many of them had also moved to the area for employment with the Atchison Topeka and Santa Fe, and they all relied on each other like family.

During the winter months, it was harder working outdoors. Ida had to be extra diligent about dressing the children properly. They had not experienced these kinds of cold temperatures down near the Gulf of Mexico. Neighbors warned them the dry cold could give them a false sense of security. Down in Louisiana with the high humidity, the cold felt much colder than it actually was. It seemed to chill you to the bone. It was not the same in the drier climate in the mountains of Colorado. You could actually become hypothermic before you realized it, especially young children who would not understand what was happening to them.

After a long, brutal winter, Murphy Chester made his grand appearance on April 30, 1921. Not only were his parents elated at this tiny new addition, Marvin, Mildred, and even little Sim were enamored for their latest sibling. Even with the extra work load and extra mouth to feed, Mid and Ida could not have felt more blessed. He grew with and became another important and viable member of the family.

Mid worked for the railroad company until the O. R. E. went on strike in 1923. That is when the Atchison Topeka and Santa Fe hired non-union workers, "Scabs," and Mid was out of work. He reverted to his skills in the timber industry and hired on at LaJunta Camp No. 8, a local sawmill. His skills with that line of work were evident, but he wanted to earn more money for his expanding family. They decided to rent a cheaper house at 1305 Grace Street.

It was a lot of work to relocate, but they had no choice. At least it was early summer, which made it easier. Of course the children did not mind because Mid and Ida convinced them it was an adventure. They explained that they would have more room to play in the yard because it was not located in downtown like the one they had. Although it was quite a chore to haul water, the family transitioned well to the new house.

As soon as Mid got word that the Denver & Rio Grande Railroad (D&RG) were hiring workers in Salida, they made plans to move there. First, Mid would ride the rails to Salida and apply for a job. If he were fortunate enough to be hired, he would scout a place to rent for the family and send for them later. Ida and the children did not want to see him leave, but what other choice did they have? Ida plaited her hair and prayed.

Ida with Marvin, Sim, Mildred, Murphy

LaJunta, Colorado 1923

6

Mid left LaJunta on August 18, 1923 and arrived in Salida the same day. The D&RG was happy to hire him, so he looked around town for a house to rent. He located and acquired one at 221 East First Street, next door to the Rainbow Hotel. His plan was to save enough money to move his family there as quickly as possible.

During their weeks-long separation, Ida held on to a poem she had writtern during her younger days before she married and would read it often. It gave her comfort.

FOR EVERY GOOD AND PERFECT GIFT IS FROM THE HOLY GIVER

Ida Williams

I thank Thee Father for all thou givest

For friends, for loved ones

and Jesus who loved us dearest

Father, I thank Thee for the Springtime that brings

the bright warm day, the flowers that bloom, the birds that sing

And the many other wonderful and beautiful things

The dear old winter days are coming when all about it cold

Then is my warmest love for every human soul

The summer days are drawing to an end

If there is any good that we can do

Now is the time to begin.

In the meantime, they exchanged the following letters:

Salida, Colorado

August 22, 1923

Mrs. Higginbotham

LaJunta, Colo.

Dear Sweetheart,

I will drop you a few lines again tonight to let you
know that we started to work this morning. I like the job and
the place here fine. The water here is wonderful. Lots of tall

mountains all around that goes clear above the clouds. You can get on top and look down at the clouds. The air is sure fine here. No hard water at all. The air doesn't seem as dry here as it does in LaJunta, but you can tell some difference in the climate. But it isn't hard to get used to.

If I only had my sweetheart and the children with me it would sure be nice. I sure do hope you are all getting along well. You must write often and let me know. I sure will be lonesome Sunday. It will be at least 30 days before I can see you all again and probably longer, but I sure am glad of my job. The foremen just seem to be fine fellows from general on down.

We are getting $5.04 for eight hours work. I am going to ask them to let me work some overtime as they pay time and half for overtime. Simmons said he made $12.00 per day all last week, and if he can, I can.

I sure did get tired of looking at mountains while we were coming up here, but it isn't half bad here.

Well I will have to tell you about my little misshap last night. I had been to mail your letter and as I came back to the rooming house I had to climb a flight of stairs about 18 feet high and when I got to the top I had to make a short turn, as there was no light, I made a mis-step and lost my balance and fell clear to the bottom of the stairway, but it didn't hurt much. I bruised my right knee pritty bad and sprained my right rist but not very bad, not bad enough to keep me from work. But I consider I come out awful luckey at that. My right leg is pritty stiff and sore but not serious. I have to be pritty cautious about how I step but it is getting better fast. It hurt pritty bad at first but I had to laugh a little as I woke up everybody in the house – ha.

Sweetheart I haven't had time to look about a house yet as I think there will be plenty of time yet before I get a payday but rent is auful reasonable to what is there. Well I want to drop Frank a line so I will close with much love for you and the children. Get some "brown suga" for Dady. Tell Marvin and the rest hello for Dada and don't worry about me. I am doeing fine. Good night.

Papa

P. S. The other boys are off loafing. I am here by myself.

∎∎

Salida, Colo.

August 24, 1923

Dear little Marvin and Mama.

Papa got your letters today and was sure glad to hear from you. Dady sure is lonesome for you tonight. Dady hopes you are having a good time. Was sorry to hear of the river being up again. Dady will have to wait until he can get a payday before he can see you all again.

Dear Mama. Your letter was so sweet and kind. I felt so much better since I heard from you. You must take care of yourself and not worry about me. I will be as careful as possible as my whole heart is with my dear little family.

I am sure glad you have company to stay with you at night.

Well Mama, I guess you had as well get what you can out of the stuff but keep the mattresses and quilts as we will need them up here. It may be the 1st of October before we can get ready to move as my payday will be rather small the first time.

I will have to wait until the 15th of Sept. before I can come home to see you again as I will not have any money to pay my way from Pueblo to LaJunta. I can get a pass to Pueblo but will have to pay my way from there on as it will be off of the D&RG System.

I only have $1.00 left now as I had to buy me some underwear and a shirt & hat and a pair of socks and paid 2 weeks room rent and paid my part on the gas & oil. Up here then we had to eat 2 days off of it before we could draw a meal ticket from the company, so I guess that was pritty good for so small amount to start with.

Mama if you get any letters from Frank or anyone down there just put them in with your letters and send them to me please.

Well I guess I will close as I have no news of interest. Would sure like to be with you tonight and tomorrow. Best wishes, I am as ever

Papa

∎∎∎

(Only part of the following letter was found.)

…..They give us all we can chamber 3 times a day. It is almost like being in LaJunta to be here, there is so many fellows from there working here. If you see Brownnie tell him they are still hiring men here. He may get a job if he wants to come up. They would have put on several more men the day we began if they could have gotten them.

Mama I sure feel lonesome for you and the kids but if you are worrying just quit it. I think we will make it all right. Just get out among other people and have a good a time as possible.

If you have a chance to talk to Mr. Spicer, tell him I got me a good job up here, but may not be able to pay him very much until October 1st as I won't get a very big pay check the first time.

Well I will close with the dearest love to you and all the children. May God bless and keep you all safely and guide our footsteps that we may ….

From Papa

Salida, Colo.

August 31, 1923

Mrs. J. M. Higginbotham

My dear wife. I received your letter this noon and read it with much pleasure, also Marvin's letter. Was sure glad to note that you were all getting along well. I am as well as common. I have felt fine today. I hope you all enjoyed your chicken. I wish my eats was as cheap as you say yours has been. It is costing me about $6.00 or $7.00 per week and then I don't have what I would like to eat.

I have just been talking to the old landlady about renting two furnished rooms and she says she will let us have them if the other people don't come back pritty soon. They will cost us $14.00 per month furnished, so if I rent furnished rooms you can just sell everything but the quilts and mattresses. You may as well sell the sewing machine too as it will cost more to pay the freight on it up here than it will be worth. I am thinking now that they will be laying off a lof of men here before Spring and if they do we will get a pass over the D&RG down in Texas and then we will buy a ticket on to where we want to go. But please don't tell anybody about what I am thinking of doing whatever you do. For I don't like Salida for a permanent home as it is too wild for me.

If I can get this place where we are rooming it will be a nice place to stay and this old lady seems to be auful nice old woman and she has a lawn and shade trees also.

Well Mama I will close for the present. Will write again tomorrow. Answer soon Sweetheart and tell little Marvin to write. Tell all the children hello for papa and get some "brown suga" offen Hick for dada. God bless their little hearts. Goodnight.

From Papa

■■■

Salida, Colo.

September 2, 1923

Mrs. J. M. Higginbotham

Dear Wife. I will write you a few lines tonight, hope they will find you all well and enjoying yourselves. Mama I guess you were all awful lonesome today. I worked today and am pretty tired tonight. I am afraid it is going to be awful hard to rent a house here as it seems like. People are having an awful hard time trying to find a place to stay. I am afraid now we will have to rent at LaJunta a while yet, but Mama I am going to try awful hard when I get a payday to get a house up here. Maybe somebody will move out and we can get a place to stay at anyway. Oh gee, I hope so as I am getting awful tired of batching allready. If I can't find a place to stay I will stick it out here as long as possible and when I get enough ahead to pay our way to Houston, we will just get up and leave this place. Well Mama I will have to lay off tomorrow. I am going to wash me out some clothes if nothing happens.

Mama, when I get a payday I will send you some money and let you pay up your grocery bill and get you some new clothes for yourself and the children if you can. I guess you will have to pay some on the rent too. I will do my best to send you $20.00 or $25.00 dollars. I will have to keep a little to pay room rent and get me another change of clothes. I will only draw $33.86 next payday as my pie ticket cost me $10.00. I only got in nine days on last month. The whole thing would amount to $45.96.

Well Mama, I am short on paper tonight so I will have to cut this letter short so answer soon and all the news. With much love to you all.

From Papa

P. S. I would like to have a sweet kiss from you all tonight.

Mama, you may get two letters at once this time but if you do I hope you will enjoy reading them.

■■

Salida, Colorado

Sept. 15, 1923

Mrs. J. M. Higginbotham

LaJunta, Colo.

My dear wife. I will write you a few lines tonight.
Hope you are all well. I am well but pretty tired.

Mama, I had to work overtime this evening and the
post office was closed and I didn't get to send you any money
in this letter but I will mail it to you Monday morning and you
will get it Tuesday. I am afraid to risk it in this letter as it
might be lost, so will be best to play it safe.

Mama I sure hate to disappoint you this time but I
couldn't do any better so please don't think hard of me.

Well Mama I got the two rooms all right but had to pay
2 weeks rent on them this evening, which amounted to $7.00.
I have $20.00 left to send to you. My payday was only $33.61
this time and I had to get me a suit of overalls and a under suit
and some sox to keep from going naked. Allthough I will
draw $68.78 next payday clear of all expenses.

Well Mama I feel good to know that I am safe on the rooms and just as quick as your passes comes I will mail them right to you so you can come right on so you can be with me.

So I will close with best wishes and many kisses.

From Papa

■■

Salida, Colorado

September 17, 1923

Mrs. J. M. Higginbotham

1305 Grace Street

LaJunta, Colo.

My dear wife. I will write you a few lines tonight. Hope they will find you all well. I am as well as common. I didn't go out on the wrecker today, I worked on the rip track so I only got 8 hours today.

Well Mama I got me a little bunch of groceries tonight and started to batching. Me and Green is in together. My supper cost me about 25 cents tonight where it has been costing me 40 cents, so my food bill now will be about 75 cents per day.

Well Mama, I have decided to have you sell the mattresses and sewing machine and everything but the quilts and pillows. It will cost us more to ship it up here than it will be worth. And then, we won't have room for the extra junk no way. So just sell it for as much as you can get out of it, but keep the quilts and pillows, and when we get straightened out again we can get something new.

If you can get up money enough out of the stuff you can come up any time you wish, but if you want to wait until the passes come you can. Of course the passes will save you about $6.00 on the fare.

I will suggest that you sell it right away with the understanding that you could use it until the passes gets there, and then all you will have to do will be to catch the train and beat it up here. Mama I sure do want to see you and the children. I am sure tired of tuffing it out without you. And everything is ready now to receive you. The only thing left to do is for you to get here and then my prayers will be answered. So do all you can to be ready when the time comes.

You won't hardly notice any difference in the climate here, I doubt if you notice it at all. It might give you the

headache for a day or two but it won't last long. So I must
close for this time with best wishes. I am as ever,

Papa

P. S. I sent you $20.00 this morning. did you get it? hope so.

■■

LaJunta, Colo.

September 18, 1923

Mr. J. M. Higginbotham

Salida, Colorado

My dear Husband. I answer your kind letter read
yesterday with much pleasure. We are well and hope you are
too well Papa. It is still cloudy and cold but hope it will clear
off soon.

Well you have been up thire 4 weeks today and it
doesent seem so long to us but I guess it has been long to you.
Well Papa I dident get the money yesterday but maby I will
today.

Little Hick said "I want write to Daddy so if you cant read it just say he ment "Gugves"? – and Sim wanted to write so Dady you can just guess at what they ment. Well dear Joe I will try to finish this letter. I got the money you sent or that is, the money order today which I am thankful for. I am afraid you dident keep enough for yourself. Well Dady, will I have to bring the cotton bed or is the room got bed? I haven't sold the sewing machine yet, can't find anyone wants to buy it. Guess I will have to ship it as I don't want to give it away or go off and leave it here. I will always need a machine. But if I see anyone who will buy it I will sell it.

My! but it is COLD!! I will pay Mr. Spicer all I can but do you want me to bring my dishes? Or have you got them furnished? Well I will close for this time with much love and worry.

From Ida

Higginbotham

Salida, Colorado

Saturday night,

September 22, 1923

Dear Mama and children

I received your letter today and was sure glad to hear from you all again. Was sorry you didn't feel very well. Hope you feel better now. I am as well as common. I have to work again tomorrow. Wish I could work tonight for a few hours anyway.

Mama, I sure am tired of trying to batch. Green wont do a durn thing toward helping me keep the rooms clean. I sure am tired of him. Will be so glad when you arrive to cook me a good meal. You wont have such a hard time Mama when you get up here as you wont have to break your back drawing water and you won't have so many big dirty rooms to clean up and your cooking will be easier because things are handier. You have your hydrant right in the kitchen. Well Mama I will give you a line up on when to leave LaJunta and when you will arrive here – here it is:

Leave LaJunta at 2:15 PM in the evening, arrive at Pueblo 4:30 PM, Leave Pueblo at 8:30 PM on train No 3. Arrive Salida at 11:30 PM. Now Mama, these are the connections you want to make. You will have to lay over at

Pueblo 4 hours as you can't ride train No 1 and train No. 2 on a pass, and Dada will meet you at the depot and bring you home. If you do happen to come when I am not looking for you, you will find your rooms at 221 East First Street, next house to the Rain Bow Hotel on the same side of the street. You can just inquire for the Rain Bow Hotel then just pass by it and the next hours is where you will find me. (note: East of the Rain Bow) Inquire for Mrs. Withems Rooming House, 221 East First St. You keep this letter for you will need it as it contains valueable information for you. If there is anything written here that you don't understand let me know and I will try to make it plainer if I can. Now I will tell you again so you cant missunderstand me. Leave LaJunta on the "Plug" at 2:15 oclock, arrive Pueblo at 4:30 PM. Leave Pueblo on No. 3 at 8:30, arrive at Salida at 11:30 PM that night and I will meet you. You see Mama, you arrive here the same day as you leave LaJunta.

So as I am tired I will close with best wishes and eagerly awaiting your arrival as I need you Mama. So answer soon. Will close with love.

From Papa

■■■

Ida followed Mid's instructions per his letter dated September 22, 1923. She and the four children left the following week. The steam train traveled beside the Arkansas River and wound through the steepest mountains Ida had ever seen! Even though she had grown up in the mountains of Arkansas, the mountains east of Salida were much rockier and jagged. She marveled at their splendor and pointed them out to the children. Their eyes widened with excitement and wonder.

Long hours later when they arrived in Salida, Mid was waiting on them at the depot. It was almost midnight. Though they were tired and sleepy, their adrenaline kicked in, and they grabbed and hugged each other tight; they had not seen each other in over a month. Mid grabbed little Murphy ("Hick") who was sleeping, and Ida directed Marvin, Mildred, and Sim toward Mrs. Withems Rooming House at 221 East First Street, next-door to the Rainbow Hotel and about a quarter-mile from the train station. What a relief and blessing to be back together!

The happy couple worked hard at reestablishing themselves and their young family. Ida certainly enjoyed having water available inside her new kitchen. No more hauling water! With the high altitude, it had really been a struggle for her when Mid had been away those weeks. *Life will be so much easier here,* she thought. *At least our family is back together like it should be!*

The following day when Mid showed them around town, Ida was pleased at the sights. Both horses and buggies, along with Model A and Model T automobiles, lined the pristine streets in downtown. Tenderfoot Mountain rose in splendor above the community. Hustling and bustling shoppers lined the sidewalks on both sides of the roads. With travelers arriving periodically on the passenger trains and workers going to and from their jobs, it was a very lively town.

Originally, the town of Salida was named "South Arkansas" when the D&RG Railroad reached the area in 1880. Later it was renamed Salida, the Spanish word for "exit," because it represented the exit to the Arkansas River canyon. The surrounding mountains made it a very alluring site for residents and visitors alike.

There was a nice park area where residents could lounge under the shade of large cottonwood trees. It was a great place for families to take their picnic lunches and let their children play. Mid and Ida took advantage whenever he was off work and they could do so. Occasionally, Mid would play his harmonica or fiddle.

At the end of the park, the picturesque F Street Bridge provided access to those who needed to cross the Arkansas River toward the train station. The concrete, arched bridge was an extravagant engineering masterpiece. It also allowed residents and visitors to stand on the bridge and observe river activity. The views were spectacular! The family thoroughly enjoyed the times they were able to spend there.

In earlier days there had been two wooden suspension bridges, one at F Street and another one a little downstream. There were problems, however. Every so often, floods would obliterate the bridges, and they would have to be rebuilt. During a 1904 Memorial Day celebration honoring Union soldiers who had died at sea, many onlookers made their way to the middle of the bridge located downstream to observe the launching of a ship covered with flowers. As they began tossing flowers into the fast-moving spring waters, a cable broke. Suddenly, the currents swept the bridge out from under them. Most of them were rescued except for a woman and three children, who perished.

One day while Ida was tending to Murphy and cleaning on the house, Marvin, Mildred and Sim slipped outside and around back of their house. There was a small pond located nearby. When they spied a large wash tub, they had the bright idea of using it as a boat and sailing across the pond in it. Of course the tub sank! Fortunately, a nearby neighbor saw what was happening and helped rescue them. Ida was beside herself. More than ever, she wanted to make sure her children had better memories of their childhood than the ones that still haunted her after all those long years.

Even though the school year had already begun, they were able to enroll Marvin and Mildred into their appropriate classes. Sim would not be old enough to attend until the following year. That would leave only two children for Ida to watch after while Mid and the others were away.

The Higginbotham family's time together there was short-lived. They had only settled in Salida for about six months before learning the Denver Rio & Grande would lay off many of their workers. Apparently, this happened annually.

Mid mailed a letter to his brother Frank, explaining his predicament. In a return letter Frank convinced him there was plenty of work in Houston, especially with the new oil refinery in Beaumont. He explained that some neighbor boys had been hired at $6.00 per day. Frank even offered to borrow the money for Mid to pay their passage. He explained that he and Simon could work together to help Mid pay off the note. Since Mid's cough had all but vanished, the family decided to head south to Houston.

In the spring of 1924 when railroad workers were laid off, they were able to get free passage on the D&RG passenger line as far as it ran in that direction. Then they had to purchase tickets for the remaining distance on into Houston. Though they knew not what lay ahead for them, their *faith* in God *and* their *hope* for their future gave them the courage to move on. Besides, they would be closer to family.

7

The train ride south was long and arduous, especially with four small children. Walking from one train car to another in order to access the restroom was challenging, and the clickety-clack of the tracks was never-ceasing. The restroom was exceptionally tiny, and it made it difficult for Mid and Ida to help their small children in such a tight space. Due to the constant movement, it was hard to stand still without holding onto something.

Thankfully, there was a dining car and an observation deck near the rear of the train where they could stretch their legs occasionally. In spite of this, it seemed another adventure for the children. Marvin, Mildred, Sim, and Hick had no concerns in the world. Their full trust lay with their parents who had always provided for their needs.

Arriving in Houston, the family was met by family members, where they stayed temporarily. Mid was able to acquire different jobs, one of which was laying bricks on Harrisburg and Navigation Streets. This was when many roads were paved with bricks. Since they owned no automobile, he had to walk to and from work.

It wasn't long until Ida realized she was with child once again. Here they were barely scratching by a living for the six of them with no stable employment for Mid, and she was carrying another baby. It seemed too much to bear. *What were they going to do?*

Finally, in 1925 Mid was able to find a permanent job at the Koppers Wood Preserving Unit, a creosote plant located on the north side of Collingsworth Street where the Houston,

East and West Texas Railroad (later the Southern Pacific) and the Houston Belt & Terminal Railroad crossed. His beginning salary was only $12 per week, so they had a tough time making ends meet.

With a stable job, however, the family was able to purchase a house at 812 Henley Street in the Brooke Smith Addition located on the north side of Houston, near North Main and close to the Heights area. Mid paid monthly notes on the place, and the couple prepared for the arrival of another baby. Milton Joseph was born that August 18th.

The family was happy there for three years until someone came along with a second lien they knew nothing about. The family was forced to leave, losing all of their investments. Mid and Ida were in disbelief! How could someone do that to them? They had poured so much of their time, energy, and money into this place! Ida cried uncontrollably. More than anything she wanted her own children to have a better life than the one she had had growing up. Poor Mid tried his best to console her, but his efforts were futile. He turned his anger into determination. If it took the rest of his life, he was not going to let her down.

Fortunately, they found a place to rent near Airline Drive and Little York Road on the north side of Houston. Although it originally had been a large chicken coop, it had been converted into a one-room house. It was owned by the Joseph Canino family who operated the large farm where it sat. It certainly was not the place of their dreams, but they had to make it work until they could legitimately buy their own place. And next time they would make sure there were no liens on it!

Living in such cramped conditions did not allow room inside for visitors, so they would usually visit outside during good weather. However, when Ida learned her mother needed someone to help care for her, she took her in. Even though her mother had not seen to Ida's needs properly as a young girl, Ida had forgiven her and felt it was her Christian duty.

The Converted Chicken House

Mid & Ida on porch

Hallie & family with little Milton

Fall 1928

Marvin playing Mid's fiddle (Fall 1928)

All of the Higginbotham children eventually acquired nicknames. Milton was dubbed "Boonie" for the rest of his life, and Mildred was usually referred to as "Sister." With Boonie's older siblings all attending school, this was a blessing on the family, not only for the good of the children and their education, but because they were so crowded in this extremely small house. Mid and Ida visited with family as often as possible, but there just was not room for everyone to come inside if the weather happened to be unfavorable. Most of their visiting took place outdoors. Besides, this place did not belong to them.

The family were forced to live in these cramped conditions until 1930 when they were finally able to purchase two acres in the Woodsdale Addition, located about two miles east of the Canino place. The land sat two blocks north of Little York Road between Aldine-Westfield and Humble Road (now Interstate 69), and there were only a couple of houses in that area at the time. It was a rural area on the outskirts of Houston.

Every payday, Mid would buy all the lumber they could afford, and he began building their new house. When they finished drying in one room, they moved inside. They took with them chickens and a cow they had already been raising on the Canino farm. With very meager means, the family pushed forward, and Mid became quite the carpenter. As he continued working on the house, he honed his craft and became rather creative.

The stock market had recently crashed, and the Great Depression had begun. With little cash on hand, they bartered for things they could not pay for. Since Mid was determined to provide his sweetheart with a water well so she would not have to haul water from long distances, and they did not have enough cash to pay for one, he bartered some of his chickens for that service. The agreed upon cost was one chicken per one foot of well. Mid had a 33 foot well dug and paid 33 chickens for that amenity. He also built a small privy out behind the house.

The children were enrolled and attending the Luther Burbank School located at the corner of Tidwell and Beauman Roads. Mr. Barrak was the principal at that time. The children seemed to do well in school, but Sim was the one to excel academically.

The school bus would pick up the children at the end of the road and drop them back off in the same location after the school day, so they had to walk to the bus stop in the mornings and walk from the bus stop home in the afternoons. The bus had wooden seats running its length on both sides. In the center was a double row of wooden benches that also ran the length of the bus. Children would sit back-to-back in the center seats. Although the seats had backs to lean against, there were no cushions for comfort and no seatbelts for safety.

One day as they were walking home from the bus stop, a car pulled alongside the children on the muddy road, and a man, with his arm extended out the window, grabbed Mildred by the arm and yanked her up onto his running board. As he was trying to accelerate, Marvin and Sim ran and grabbed her and pulled her away as the man sped off. This incident unnerved everyone in the neighborhood, especially her family. After that episode neighbors became vigilant about watching the children walk to and from the bus.

As Mid continued working on the house, he had the boys pitch in and help when they were home from school. Marvin, Sim, and Hick were old enough to assist him, but Boonie was a bit too young. He was not quite school age, so he and Mildred helped their mother inside when they could. The family worked hard together to continue building the house and making life there more comfortable.

When Mildred was eight years old, she was given the job of shaving her father with a straight razor. After a hard day's work at the plant, he enjoyed leaning back and relaxing in a chair while she practiced, then perfected her craft. Mid would always encourage her and compliment the job she was doing.

Eventually, she began giving the boys haircuts with the hand-powered clippers. They had no electricity at the time. As more people moved into the neighborhood, Mildred began giving free haircuts to many of them. She even received a Bible from the preacher after she cut his hair.

Even though Mid had a push-plow, he owned no mule or horse, so he did all the hard pushing himself in order to plow up the garden area behind their house. This was no small task! The soil was dark and rich and perfect for growing crops, but it was also mixed with a lot of clay. Since the Houston area received tons of moisture and rain from the nearby Gulf of Mexico, this became extremely difficult and messy during wet times. The dirt would form thick muck and stick to anyone's shoes or feet. When it dried, it was like clumps of hard concrete that had to be knocked off. However, his beautiful and tasteful corn, squash, peas, cantaloupes, and watermelons were the pay-off.

On top of all this hard work, Mid continued walking several miles to work every weekday at the creosote plant and then another several miles back to their house. They simply could not afford an automobile at the time.

After Boonie started school, Ida filled her days cooking and cleaning, but she also found time to plant and tend to strawberries and sew clothes for the children from beautifully decorated feed sacks. She also stitched her famous quilts. In fact, she would have quilting parties with some of the ladies from church.

Mid and Ida were charter members for the Woodsdale Baptist Church. It was located at the corner of Little York Road and Sommerset Lane. That is where they attended most Sundays and where all of their children eventually were baptized into Christ. Ida would often read scriptures from the Bible to them. They wanted to instill in their children the same values and work ethic with which they had been blessed by Mid's family. Without their strong faith, they would not have survived the hardships and struggles they had had to endure, and they wanted to pass that same faith on to their descendants.

Finally, Mid and Ida's little home on a rural route north of downtown Houston was transforming into their own small paradise. Whenever Mid could find a few free minutes, he would sit out on the porch and play his harmonica and fiddle and really appreciate the fruits of all their hard labor. All of their children could proudly attend school and know they had their own home in which to return at the end of the day. Even though the Great Depression raged on, the Higginbothams' small neighborhood grew, and the church friends and neighbors became an important extension of their own family and an integral part of their lives. They all depended on each other.

8

As the boys grew older, they would hunt rabbits and squirrels in the nearby woods and Hall's Bayou that ran not far behind their place. This helped provide the family with meat to go with the delicious vegetables and fruits that were grown.

Mid bartered for some pigs and began raising them. After his litter grew and began reproducing, he would, with the help of his sons, slaughter and process a couple of them for meat. This was no small or pleasant task! It had to be performed during cold weather, and the boys were not thrilled when they were told it was "hog-killing time." But they pulled up their boots and waded into the pig pen and did their job, and there certainly was no complaining at the breakfast table when their mother placed fried bacon or sausage on the table to complement their eggs and biscuits.

During the Great Depression, it seemed the folks in town suffered far more than the folks in rural areas. At least the Higginbotham family were able to provide for their basic necessities, and the children were unaware of the suffering in other parts of the country. As far as they were concerned, they were healthy and happy most of the time, and they were unaware of the emotional struggles their parents were facing. All they realized were the physical aspects of the hard work they witnessed.

One day Marvin ran into the house screaming! When he had visited the privy out behind the house, he was bitten on the buttocks by a snake. Alarmed, Mid and Ida examined him. They were not sure what kind of snake it was, whether it was poisonous or not. Quickly, Ida made a poultice from a piece of salted bacon and placed it on his bite. This prompted Mid to move the outhouse to another location. From then on he would occasionally move the privy to a different spot.

The family had been surviving the worst aspects of the Depression for about four years when Ida began showing signs of menopause. Her moods fluctuated many times, and the emotional scars from her childhood began to rear their ugly heads. Because the boys spent more time with their father now, she convinced herself that they did not love her as much as they loved him. Her insecurities were evident. She was despondent and would often cry while she plaited her hair. She just could not understand why the boys she bore seemed to enjoy spending more time with their father than with her. It did not occur to her that they were learning from their dad how to become men.

And Mildred was exhibiting signs of that teenage independent streak. By then Mid and Ida had finally been able to purchase their first car, a Pontiac. When Mildred began dating, her parents would follow behind to keep an eye on her. Of course this caused resentment in their only daughter.

Ida was 42 years old now and it was not long before she had the hard realization that she was pregnant again. *I can't be pregnant again! Not now!* Marvin was 19, Mildred 16, Sim 15, Hick 13, and Boonie nine years old. Marvin and Mildred had already dropped out of school and were working. Mildred had a job next to the Kress Dime Store in downtown Houston. Because she had grown up with four brothers, she so badly wanted a little sister.

Mid tried comforting and reassuring Ida, but he also wondered how in the world they could afford another child. He was just thankful they had finished building the house. Even though it was not a large house, they would make it work. It was times like these his *faith and hope* shone through the brightest and became an inspiration to those around him. On the cold 23rd day of February 1934, their fifth son made his appearance. Ida had just turned 43 the previous month. Since her parents realized Mildred was hoping for a girl, they gave her naming privileges. She chose Maurice Edwin for him. Later he acquired the nickname "Scooter."

Marvin, Sim, Murphy, Scooter, Mildred, Boonie

1934

Scooter's older siblings were infatuated with the little fellow. As their baby brother grew, the older boys loved picking at him. There had always been competition between the older boys to see who could get one off on the others, but now they had another brother to include in their antics. One time it was placing a slice of rubber cheese in with the real cheese and waiting to see who the victim would be. It might be pulling the covers off one of the boys after they had gone to bed. Other times it would be farting in the other's face or walking by and releasing an SBD, Silent But Deadly, one near their latest victim. This went on and on. Apparently, it made their hard life a little more bearable.

Each of the siblings developed their own personalities and interests. Marvin loved shooting his guns and making his own bullets. He became quite accomplished with his marksmanship, which would serve him well in his future assignments. One day as his siblings watched, he raised his pistol and took aim at a housefly that had just landed. The fly was obliterated. Shocked by his accuracy and what had just happened, they erupted in laughter.

Mildred was the nurturer because she was always taking care of the rest of the family, especially if they were sick or hurting. She loved the times she spent shaving her dad or cutting the boys' hair or comforting her mother when she was upset. It was her nature to try and solve problems that arose. Her family really loved and appreciated her for that. That trait served her family and neighbors well but did not help with her business dealings years later. Because she was so pretty, she was very popular with the boys. In 1936 she was one of five girls chosen out of over 100 applicants to dance in the Texas Centennial celebration held at the San Jacinto Battleground. Mildred was also an accomplished seamstress and had sewn her own beautiful dress for the occasion. Scooter remembered fondly the times she would bring toys and candy home for him.

Sim was the best educated of the family, as well as the perfectionist. Everything had to be done the correct way. This trait would definitely be an asset later on. This certainly did not mean he had no sense of humor. All of the Higginbotham children had that ingrained in them. Life was not fun unless you made it fun! That was their motto.

Murphy was the comedian in the family. He was always making the family laugh or pulling jokes on them. He earned two nicknames, "Hick" and "Mutt." Even if he were feeling down, he would try to make the others laugh. This trait certainly helped him survive some rough times, but it wasn't enough to get him through the toughest years that lay ahead.

Boonie loved to draw, especially cartoon characters. He was also a jokester like the others. Running into the house all excited one day, he told Mildred a man had hung himself. When she bolted outside, she saw a dummy he had thrown over the phone line. He was always concocting some scheme to play on his siblings. That backfired on him later because Scooter was learning from the rest of them.

One day Boonie came home rubbing his eyes. They had been bothering him all day. He reached into the medicine cabinet where he had seen one of the older brothers place a bottle of eye drops he had been given by the ophthalmologist. He dropped some into both eyes. Not realizing these were dilating drops, his vision started blurring, and he became alarmed. Reaching back into the medicine cabinet and retrieving the bottle of drops he had used, he handed it to Scooter and asked him to see what kind of drops those were.

"My God, Boonie, did you put this in your eyes!?"

It scared poor Boonie to death until Scooter started laughing, and he realized he had been pranked by his baby brother.

There were also many humorous occasions that none of them had planned or had a part of; they were just naturally occurring events. It was if nature itself was getting a few good ones over on the boys. Mid had bartered for a few ducks and a few rabbits to raise. One afternoon when Scooter was sitting on his swing, he was observing their rooster who had mounted one of their hens. One of the ducks happened to be strolling by when the rooster, who hadn't noticed it, released himself from the hen. Perfect timing for the duck. Before the

70

poor rooster knew what had happened, the duck spied what he thought was a big worm and grabbed it! Squawking and flapping, the rooster yanked himself loose from what he thought was the hen. He flapped his way up and perched on the fence, glaring down at the hen, traumatized. *What did she just do to me?*

Another time, Mutt was lying in bed attempting to go to sleep. All of a sudden, he yelled out, "What the hell was that?" A big rat had just crawled across his face and drug its nuggets right over his eyeballs. Of course, the other boys would not let him live that one down!

Because the house was set on pier and beams, their dog made a habit of sleeping under the house in the cool dirt. During warm weather, everyone would sleep with the windows raised to allow the breezes to keep it cool inside. It was deathly quiet one night when Mid let out a loud fart that terrified the dog. It jumped up, hitting his head on a beam. His yelp and barking caused a chain reaction throughout the neighborhood and on into the distance. Scooter said before the night was over every dog in Houston had barked. It was the fart heard across Houston.

Marvin decided it was time for him to find employment but could find none due to the raging Depression, so he signed up with the Army in May 1937. At that time the Army had not yet motorized to any great extent, and the artillery was still pulled by horses, and the United States had not yet been drawn into the war. After discharging from that unit, he reenlisted with the Army Air Corps in May 1940.

Because he was such a crack-shot with pistols and rifles, he was assigned as an instructor on their rifle range.

Once when Marvin was home on leave, Scooter watched him shoot the tail feathers off their old rooster with a .22 caliber H & R nine-shot revolver at a distance of about 50 feet. While the old rooster was eating scratch, Marvin began clipping the tail feathers from the top down without ever hitting the rooster.

Another time he shot the clothes pins off the clothes line while they swayed in the wind without ever hitting the clothes. Of course Ida made him buy her some more clothes pins.

In 1939 Mid decided to destroy the old outhouse and build a bigger, better one. He had honed his carpentry craft after building their house and decided to go all out on this one. It was an impressive two-holer. If someone had an emergency, they could get in there with someone else. In the center he installed a vent pipe and surrounded it with 6-inch board strips to hide the pipe. He even put wallpaper on the inside walls to make it prettier. On the door he placed a moon-shaped cut-out for final touches.

Twenty six years later, Scooter, who had been working for the Houston Belt & Terminal Railroad, typed a letter on a blank train order paper to Mildred expressing his nostalgia about this old privy.

October 12, 1965

Dear Mildred,

It is with a bit of sadness and nostalgia that I note the recent retirement and burning of our magnificient old toilet which gave 26 years of faithful service.

This was the end of an era, like the passing of the steam engine in favor of the diesel and the kerosene lamp in favor of the electric light bulb.

One of my most vivid memories of early childhood was of Paw building the old privvey back in 1939 when I was 5 years of age. - Unlike Our less fortunate neighbors, whose toilets only provided them an unsightly place to hide while they crapped, Ours was a handsome building Sort of a prestiege symbol., a Two-hole-er (one being slightly larger for the larger members of the family) featuring air tight, hinged lids, a vent pipe to the ceiling (an escape for the aroma), small screened windows near the top and neatly trimmed inside complete with gaily decorated wall-paper.

I remember Virginia Aldridge kidding Paw that she wanted to try it out when he finished building it. I couldn't help thinking that she would cover both holes at once. She was rather large. Also I smoked my first cigarette in it, (this is probably the reason I couldn't understand at the time why other people liked to smoke because the cigarettes seemed to have a some-what shittey taste), anyway Stanley Lenneburg, James Edwards and I used to hide there to smoke and at the sound of approaching g feet-steps We would g frantically fan the air to disipate the tell-tale smoke. This was one of the finest outdoor toilets in the world, among the first built in our neighborhood and the very last to go. Sad, Sad, indeed.

Your sentimental brother, Scooter.

Since jobs were still scarce in the fall of 1939, Sim and Mutt decided to enlist in the Conservation Corps, also known as the "Tree Army." Sim wrote home about his experiences in Carlsbad Caverns. They worked in New Mexico and Arizona until the following October, 1940. That is when they both enlisted in the Army together, being promised they could remain in the same outfit. Of course, that did not happen!

At first they were both assigned to Dodd's Field at Ft. Sam Houston in San Antonio. Both wrote home about the terrible food. Sim wrote home on Nov. 27, 1940: "I guess you all heard about the tragadies at Dodds Field. They say that 500 of the boys got food poisoning and I heard that from 7 to 31 of them died. But thank the Lord, we had already left

73

there. The grub was really terrible there but so far we have ate like kings over here. It happened the morning after we left."

Murphy also wrote home: "Well everything is allright here, but Dodds Field is hell. Mud is shoe top deep and everything else to make it hell!! They was dying like rats yesterday, but thank the Lord, we got out just in time. Here, I sleep in a bed and eat everything that is good. The mess hall is in tents at Dodds Field, and mud all in it, and the bread has green mole on it out thir. But here thirs fresh bread. I would have told you before, but I don't wont you worrying.

"Here we have fresh tost, 1 pt. milk, bakers, coffee, butter, bunds, and every thing to make a new meal.

"Well, I here one of Mollie's (Marvin's) French 75s going off about a half mile from here. We are going to git 2 bran new meshean guns soon. I may git one, I hope so." Signed: "From Mutt"

Less than a month later, in a letter home from Mutt, he explained that although he and Sim were both in the 23rd Infantry, they were not together any longer. Two months later he wrote informing them that Marvin had been assigned to Dodds Field and had visited them. The three brothers were able to go to the theater together and watch movies from time to time.

Murphy and Sim 1940

9

Ida plaited her hair with worry. They had heard reports that there was a war going on in Europe. Mid tried convincing her that things would calm down over there, and besides, it did not involve the United States. The boys would learn important skills that would help them later in finding jobs, and they most assuredly would make a better life for themselves than the one they had already struggled through.

Remembering her early and horrifying childhood, Ida began a 20 year-long journal writing project. It was a way for her to deal with what she was now facing with her sons possibly going off to war, and it was therapy for the memories from her past that continued to haunt her. She once remarked that if all the mothers in the world could get together and talk, there would never be any wars.

Things were also changing in their neighborhood. Their rural route address had been recently changed to reflect the growing suburban area, so they were given the new address of 2501 Lone Oak. More and more neighbors were moving in and building houses on their once sparsely populated street, and it was becoming a more vibrant neighborhood, complete with some interesting characters.

Scooter was six years old at the time and began making friends with some of the neighborhood boys, some of which were a little older than he. The Dentler family, who claimed to be part of the Dentler Potato Chip Company, lived directly across the street. Mrs. Dentler made a habit of standing out on her back porch much of the time and peeling potatoes, letting the peels fly out into her yard.

Her son was known to have a bit of a mean streak. Indiscriminately, he was always shooting at birds or squirrels or whatever became a target for him with his b.b. gun.

One day when Scooter met him out at the ice cream truck to buy a Popsicle from the vendor, the man was reaching over into his truck to get their treats, when the Dentler boy, who was sporting his b.b. gun, took aim and shot the man right in the back of the head. *Ping, ping, ping, ping!* The b.b. ricocheted inside the truck.

"Gosh, Damn!" The poor fellow grabbed the back of his head, writhing in pain. Scooter's eyes widened in disbelief! He bolted for his house because he did not want to be blamed for something he hadn't done, and he did not want to encounter the wrath of the injured man. Of course, the Dentler boy ran home with his weapon as quickly as he could run. The poor ice cream man never returned to Lone Oak Street again. It may have possibly been his last day in the business.

Since Mid and Ida were finally able to have electricity installed in their house, they later bought a radio so they could keep up with the news. They began hearing more ominous reports about the war in Germany. There was talk that the United States was sure to enter the war, and they both worried about the possibility of Marvin, Sim, and Mutt being shipped off to fight in a war they just did not understand. *Why would the United States get involved in a war that did not concern them?* They were still haunted by memories of the

First World War and had been so thankful their sons at that time were not old enough to enlist or be drafted into the service. Now they were faced with that very grim possibility.

They found out Marvin was going to meet his brothers at Ft. Sam Houston in San Antonio, so they planned a trip there. It would pacify them for at least a short time, and maybe they would find reassurance that everything was going to be fine.

Mutt, Hugo Stoerner, Marvin, Mid, Ida, Sim, and
Scooter in front; Ft. Sam Houston, San Antonio 1940

Mildred had begun dating Hugo Stoerner, and it
wasn't long before the family realized they were serious about
one another. When they married on January 13, 1941, it left a
hole in Ida's heart, not that she wasn't happy for her daughter,
but she was beginning to experience that empty nest
syndrome closing in on her. With the three boys off in the
military, that only left Boonie and Scooter; however, Boonie

had begun slipping off with other boys and drinking and getting into fights, so he was not always at home. This also concerned both of his parents.

While Mid worked at the creosote plant and Scooter was away at school, Ida stayed busy cooking, cleaning, quilting, or canning, just anything to keep her mind occupied. If she had too much quiet time, she would revert back to her plaiting of hair and worry.

"Japan just attacked Pearl Harbor!" December 7, 1941 made quite clear to the family that their worst fears were coming true. The whole country was reeling in shock and disbelief! Many tears flowed as family and neighbors spread the news like wildfire! People began gathering to listen to news reports and to offer prayers for the country. They just could not believe what was happening. It was a nightmare from which they could not awake.

After President Roosevelt created the Office of Price Administration, the OPA began in May of 1942 rationing tires, automobiles, oil, fuel, gasoline, coal, firewood, nylon, silk, and shoes. Americans began having scrap drives to collect needed items such as scrap metal for tanks. Tires and rubber were collected to make Jeep tires. Clothing was collected to make cleaning rags. Nylons and silk stockings were collected to make parachutes, and even left-over cooking fats were collected to make explosives for the war effort. Even though the scrap drives added little to the overall needs of the military, it galvanized the nation's morale as a whole.

Scooter was all in on these scrap drives. It gave him a sense of purpose and a way to help his brothers. He spent countless hours collecting items from the neighbors. To him his heroes were not the movie stars or sports figures of the day; they were his real-life brothers. *Why did I have to be so young? It's not fair!* But he trudged along and did all he could do. After all, what could an eight year-old boy do by himself?

Marvin and his first cousin, Dock Williams' daughter who lived in Portales, New Mexico, were married for a short time. They could not agree on whether to live in Houston or Portales, so Marvin wrote a letter home, dated August 11, 1942. In it he wrote:

"Dear Mother, Dad, Brothers and Sister

I can't send my payment this time because the Govt. took $44.00 out of my pay check to send the wife. I missed sending her the cash last month so I will send it next month. Say, is Sim a lieutenant yet? I heard he was home. I would like his address, and mutt hasen't answered my last letter for some time.

Say, the wife wants a picture of me, so if you have a few you might send her one. This married life has about got me down since nothing ever seems to go rite. I wanted the wife to stay in Houston but she would not. She never does anything I ask her to do if her folks don't want her to do it. Some day I may if I am lucky get a divorce so I could save a little dough instead of having to keep her and her folks up. Talk about a war of nerves, but this married life is worse on my nerves than the war is. Dock and his folks has a strangle hold on me now, but I will get out of it some way if I can."

Wanting to follow in his brothers' footsteps, 17 year-old Boonie enlisted in the Navy on December 14, 1942. Mid and Ida's world seemed to be falling apart. With the war raging on with no signs of finality, they were left at home with Scooter. They found out Boonie had trained as a radio-man and was assigned to the new Escort Carrier Bismark Sea, but he was later transferred to a Carrier Air Service Unit where he remained for the duration of the war. Secretly, they hoped the service would be good for him; maybe he would become more responsible and stop all the drinking and fighting.

Their hopes for him were dashed when he came in from leave and admitted to participating in a huge fight with some Zoot Suiters, one of Los Angeles' 38th Street Mexican-American teenager gangs. Because some of the Navy sailors had to cross part of their neighborhood in order to return to base after partying in town, the group attacked one of the sailors. In retribution a group of sailors attacked them. Not wanting to miss an opportunity for another drunken fight, Boonie had joined in.

As they heard more and more news reports about the war effort, Mid and Ida had a feeling their four sons would end up fighting somewhere before it was over. All they could do was hope and pray that did not happen.

Milton J. Higginbotham

Boonie wrote: To Ma and Pa and Scooter

Love to all, Boonie

10

Another family who had moved to the neighborhood was the William Sylvester Edwards family who lived on Trenton Street, the next street from Lone Oak, but three or four blocks away from the Higginbothams'. His wife Selma Johanna Kohtz Edwards and their family had moved to Houston from Peoria, Illinois in 1924 because William suffered from a bad case of asthma from the cold and coal smoke. His doctor had told him he would not live over six months if he didn't move to a different climate. Since he had relatives in Houston who had promised him a job, the family loaded up and headed south.

The Edwards family had eight children: William, Esther, Lois, Lucille, Melvin, twins Merle and Earle, and the youngest, James. James was only eight months older than Scooter, and they became good friends. They both had brothers serving during the war. James's three brothers who were serving their country were Melvin and the twins, Merle and Earle. It was common practice for military families to post stars on their door posts of their houses. The Edwards family had three stars, and the Higginbotham family had four. This connection helped form a strong bond between them.

James and Scooter spent many hours together entertaining themselves and even getting into trouble at times. When the two boys missed the school bus one day, James talked Scooter into skipping school so they could build some scooters. Of course, Scooter loved the idea as much as James, so they walked down to Long's Grocery Store and picked up some apple carts. As soon as Ida saw what they were doing and realized they had skipped school, she put an end to their project. She let the boys know in no uncertain terms they would not do that again and sent James home.

Mutt had brought a baby male raccoon in one day when he was home on leave. Mid built a really nice pen for it, and the two boys loved playing with that coon. They loved getting it out of its pen and watching it do its thing. After a rain and there was water in the ditch, the coon loved reaching down in the crawfish holes. If it were lucky, it would bring out a crawfish. The boys were amused when the coon would bring one out and wash it thoroughly before eating it. They also loved giving it sugar cubes to watch as it washed them in the water. Puzzled, the coon would keep searching for the cubes that had dissolved. The boys would crack up laughing.

The coon would follow the boys around wherever they went. As it grew older, however, it became really mean and aggressive. If the boys approached its pen, it would try to attack them. Mid had to take the coon off and either turn it loose or destroy it. The boys never knew which one he chose.

Many times they would go bicycling around the neighborhood, but they liked a little more excitement than that, so they would ride to the brahma cattle field behind the Higginbothams' house. Being adventurous boys, they loved a challenge. They would crawl through the fence but not get too far away before taunting the cattle to come after them. When the cattle ran toward them, they would dive through the fence, laughing.

There were times Stanley Lonneburg, another neighbor friend, James Edwards and Scooter would hide in the fancy two-holer privy to sneak a smoke. Since Mid had installed the vent pipe, they figured no one would ever pick up on the smell of their cigarettes. Apparently, their parents were none the wiser.

After all the long, hard years Mid had worked his garden with only the power of his own muscles, he was finally able to buy a new David Bradley tractor. James and Scooter loved watching him work that machine. It was mesmerizing to watch it plow up that dark, rich dirt so easily. The boys would stay out of his way, but it was a sight to behold. You can bet these two shared stories about their brothers who were fighting overseas.

Sometimes the Dentler boys, who lived across the street, would ride up on their paint ponies. Because there was a chinaberry tree nearby, they would join in with James and Scooter and start chinaberry fights with each other. The other neighbor boys would also join in at times. During one of those fights, one of the Dentler boys stepped inside an empty garage next-door looking at the others through a knothole in the wall. One of the next-door boys who was toting his b.b. gun stepped up and shot through the hole and knocked the poor fellow's tooth out.

Scooter's parents kept a pretty tight rein on him. He was seldom allowed the freedom to run lose with the other boys when they would ride their bikes or walk back to Hall's Bayou and mess around. Because there were tons of blackberries that grew along both sides of the bayou, the other boys loved to wander around back there and pick them to eat and take home. James' mother loved to make pies out of them.

One afternoon when James was playing football with Scooter out in the front yard, the ball was accidentally thrown over the barb-wire fence that separated the next-door neighbor's place. When James went after it and was attempting to climb back through, he stumbled and fell into the wire, cutting his left arm badly.

Mid was sitting in his rocking chair on the front porch. He loved watching the boys play and would occasionally chuckle at them. He was a soft-spoken, mild-mannered man who rarely showed excitement. As the boys made their way toward him, Mid met them in the yard. Scooter told him that James was cut on the barbed wire. When Mid saw how badly it was cut, he calmly replied, "I'll go get some merthiolate."

Mid returned with a bandage sling and some merthiolate and told James, "This will probably burn." James gritted his teeth as the topical was applied. Mid wrapped his arm and told him he would drive him home. "I think it needs sewed up." He did not want to alarm James, so his voice showed no excitement.

Mid drove him home in his Pontiac and explained to his dad that he had accidentally fallen into the fence and was cut pretty badly and that he probably needed to see a doctor and have his arm sewn up. Mr. Edwards agreed and thanked him. After Mid drove off he scolded James for getting into the wire.

Mr. Edwards drove James over to see a doctor on Little York and Fontenot near the Epson Down Race Track. The doctor lived upstairs in a garage apartment and was intoxicated when they entered; however, he stitched James' arm but pulled the stitches too tight. This caused permanent scarring.

Years later James explained how much he loved Mid because he was always so nice and never got upset over things. It really impressed him how Mid had handled that situation and others without getting angry. He said he was not used to that temperament with other men.

Halls Bayou had been dredged out, with piles of dirt heaped on both sides. James and some of the other boys loved to go down there and fish. On one such occasion, James and Pete Goodman, who lived farther down Lone Oak, walked down to the bayou, intending to fish but began throwing crawfish mounds at each other.

There was a family that had placed their outdoor toilet on the bank, allowing their waste to run down into the bayou. When the boys saw the woman of the house enter the privy, they picked up crawfish mounds and bombarded the walls of the outhouse with the hard clods of dirt. Then they got the heck out of there! They were your typical American boys attempting to make a tough life more fun. After all, boys will be boys!

After James' older sister Lucille married Mutt, James and Scooter became even closer friends and spent much more time together. In fact they became life-long friends.

Sim, Mildred, Ida, Mutt

1942

Scooter 1942

11

Since Mutt had been dating James Edward's sister Lucille for a while when he joined the service, they eventually married on June 7, 1942. They had only been married five months when he got orders to transfer to Camp McCoy, near LaCrosse, Wisconsin where he would train for airborne and ski training. Because she could not stand the thought of being left behind, Lucille eventually traveled up there to be near him. She rented a room for $5.00 per week and found a job at a ladies' clothing store, but it was still 40 miles from where he was stationed.

Mutt received specialized Ranger training there. The Rangers were infantry men trained for much tougher assignments, so they practiced various maneuvers in sub-zero weather. They were reorganized by Col. William Darby and were later known as Darby's Rangers.

Mutt became good friends with Henry Albin, the Company I First Sergeant. No one under the rank of Sergeant was allowed to leave the base without a pass, but Sgt. Albin would smuggle Mutt and another friend Douglas Simpson past the guards in the trunk of his 1938 Ford Coupe. Mutt would sneak in to see Lucille whenever he had the chance. It wasn't long before she became pregnant.

When he got word he was being shipped out, Lucille caught a train back to Houston to be with family. He was shipped out of New York Harbor on October 7, 1943 aboard the troop ship S. S. Thomas H. Barry with a large convoy including a battleship and a destroyer. Air protection was also provided. The convoy sailed in a zig-zag pattern toward Ireland in order to make it more difficult for German submarines to target them. Mutt's convoy was attacked by enemy subs, but they sank three of them.

When they reached Ireland, Mutt received more training in Caledon. By mid-April, they were sent by rail back to Belfast where they embarked on a sea voyage to a marshalling area in South Wales. There they disembarked at Pembroke Dock and stayed in the "Tent City" at Haversack until they were put back aboard the ship. They stopped for a short time at Bristol Harbor but stayed on deck until they received orders to ship out to the coast of Normandy.

He was assigned to the Second Division, which was part of the planned D-Day Invasion. Specifically, they were assigned to the assault on Omaha Beach, planned for June 6, 1944; however, they missed their landing area but arrived the next day.

The men had to climb down a rope ladder in order to transfer to a smaller landing craft. The seas were really rough and there were large swells. As Mutt was climbing down, his friend below was almost down to the landing craft when a huge wave picked up the smaller boat and slammed it against the sailor, pinning him against the ship and cutting him in half. Mutt watched his friend land in the water, screaming, and disappear. Because he was afraid of the same fate, he jumped down to the boat, landing on some of the men, but they were not seriously injured. He could never shake that image from his mind, but he had to keep moving.

Like his brother Marvin, Mutt was also a crack-shot and was the number one man on the B.A.R. (Browning Automatic Rifle) team, assigned to the 23rd Infantry Regiment. His assistant was Elmer Hansen. Landing on Omaha Beach was a nightmare for them with German air raids and bombers attacking. They staggered ashore through broken and twisted steel and concrete beach obstacles and German gun emplacements which were firing on them. Mutt witnessed the great Battleship Texas engage in a duel with German shore batteries. There had been no firework display he had ever seen that compared with the tons of thundering explosives he watched that night. It was both spectacular and horrifying.

Not only was Omaha Beach the toughest landing area on Normandy, it was one of the hardest and bloodiest assault landings in military history. After Mutt's regiment landed, they were forced to wait on their vehicles in an assembly area north of St. Laurent-sur-Mer. When all of their vehicles had been unloaded, they moved north into another assembly area North of Cerisy la Foret in preparation for an attack.

The Second Division moved forward and appreciated the air support they were receiving. They were the first units to encounter the highly-trained German paratroopers, who had been primed for fighting and indoctrinated with the Nazi creed.

When the 23rd Infantry prepared to take St. Georges D'elle, Mutt was fighting through the hedgerows and had to thrust his bayonet into a young German soldier, then kick his body off the bayonet. Looking his victim in the eyes while taking his life haunted him, but he had to keep pushing forward. It was his life or theirs.

Due to the heavy artillery, Mutt was pinned down for several days. He learned that his best army buddy Jesse "Punk" Clifford, who had been fighting nearby, had been killed. It was terrifying! Occasionally, under the cover of night, supplies and mail were delivered, which gave a few minutes respite for the men. When Mutt was handed a letter and a picture from Lucille, he had to wait until dawn in order to see the photo and read her letter. It was a photograph of his beautiful baby boy, Murphy Daniel "Danny." He was overjoyed. With all the death and destruction around, it energized him to move forward and gave him a reason to succeed.

As Mutt and Elmer Hansen made their way inland and became engaged in a fierce battle for the town of St. Georges D'elle, their squad leader Sgt. Faber Overbaugh was hit in the leg by a ground burst. Elmer stayed behind to assist him. Mutt struggled forward.

After weeks of fierce fighting, Murphy was engaged in the battle for Hill 192. The real battle for that hill had been won by July 11 and finalized by the following day. His unit was then directed toward "Operation Cobra" in an effort to completely rid Normandy of German control.

Mutt was approaching the vicinity of the Souleuvre River when he was separated from his platoon. He was fighting side-by-side with Victor Barrouk when they both heard a long-range German 88 MM artillery shell coming in. Both were hit and wounded; at least two more men were killed.

Murphy was hit with a large piece of shrapnel which entered his right thigh and came out the front. Another piece entered his right shoulder. A third piece penetrated his back.

Because he was pinned down for more than 20 days, his leg injury became badly infected to the point of gangrene.

Later after Mutt was transported to a hospital, Lucille, along with Mid and Ida, received a telegram from the War Department informing them of Murphy's injuries. They were overcome with conflicting emotions. For months they had not known if he was alive or dead. On one hand they were overjoyed to know he was alive; on the other hand, they were worried he may not survive his injuries. Their worry was intense.

Lucille's brothers, Merle and Earle Edwards, had also been serving in the Navy. Merle was aboard the U. S. S. Alpine, an Assault Transport that had a landing craft used to ferry soldiers to the beach. On November 18, 1944, Merle was operating the landing craft when a Japanese suicide plane crashed into it, killing Merle. His wife Polly was seven months pregnant with their child. It had only been three months since Lucille had received word about Mutt's devastating injuries. Both families were reeling in shock and grief! They wondered if bad news would ever end. The Edwards and Higginbotham families were forged together through blood and spirit.

Merle's twin brother Earle would later marry Polly and raise Merle's daughter Elaine, along with their own three children.

Lucille & Murphy 1942

12

When Sim enlisted into the Army, he was assigned to Company C 23rd Infantry Regiment of the Second Infantry Division. Because he tested in the top two of over 200 men, he was chosen to attend Officers Candidate School. In April 1942 he was sent to Ft. Benning, Georgia where he attained the rank of Second Lieutenant the first week of July that same year. Later he was transferred to Ft. Riley, Kansas and assigned to a medical battalion and promoted to First Lieutenant in January 1943. Because he really wanted to fly, he applied for and received a transfer to the Army Air Corps as a flying cadet. This is where he successfully trained as a fighter pilot.

After receiving his "Wings" on February 8, 1944 at Foster Field in Victoria, Texas, he received three more weeks of ground school before training in the P-47 Thunderbolt. Then he was shipped to England in July aboard the famous luxury liner Queen Elizabeth. It had been commandeered for use as a troop ship during the war.

Arriving in England, Sim received more training before being assigned to the 361st Squadron, 356th Fighter Group, 67th Fighter Wing of the 8th Air Force on August 21, 1944. Their primary role was to attack strategic targets such as factories, railroads, etc. The fighter planes were to accompany the large bombers and protect them from enemy fighter planes. While Sim was in training, he developed a roll-over maneuver to escape an enemy fighter plane. The squadron leader was so impressed he began teaching this maneuver to the other pilots.

Sim was then stationed at Martlesham Heath near Ipswitch where he was also assigned "Billeting Officer" in charge of assigning new pilots to their rooms. His best friend at the time was Lt. Freeman Hooker, so he assigned him adjoining rooms. The two friends decided to combine the two rooms into one so it would be more comfortable. When a new captain arrived, he demanded Sim's room because it was much bigger, and he held rank over him. Sim refused. The captain went over his head to a superior officer but was told, "Higginbotham is the billeting officer, and you will take whichever room he assigns you."

On September 3, 1944, Sim was assigned his first combat mission. He flew into Belgium and Germany where his group of P-47s dashed into some thick clouds to escape a heavy concentration of flak bursting all around. When he came out of the clouds, he discovered that the other P-47s had disappeared, and he was over a town where he became the sole target for every anti-aircraft gun below. Somehow he managed to escape, but his plane had been hit by some of the flak, rendering his radio ineffective. He was also nearly out of fuel, and he was passing through bad weather with no visibility. His compass was the only instrument he had to guide him back to base. Just as he escaped the thick clouds, he realized he was lined up to the landing strip so he would not have to circle the field. About the time he was approaching, his engine began sputtering and died. Thankfully, he landed the aircraft safely. In his later briefing, Sim learned his squadron had attacked and destroyed 14 trains.

After his third mission over Germany, Sim received a letter from his mother informing him about Mutt's injury and his location at the hospital in Oxford. He was immediately able to get a pass to go visit him. However, he was only able to find a ride to within 25 miles of the hospital, so he had to wait until morning to catch a ride the remaining distance. About 11:00 Sim surprised Mutt when he walked into his room. It was September 12, and they were thrilled at seeing each other again and reminiscing about old times.

Because Mutt was hospitalized a few months, Sim was able to visit with him often. Thankful for the newly discovered penicillin, Mutt was able to fully recover from the gangrene. Even after Mutt was released from the hospital, the brothers would get passes and go out on the town together.

On September 17, 1944, Sim was flying his fourth mission over Holland. There were over 1500 planes and 478 gliders carrying 34,000 men. Sim told his family, "I guess you know about the Airborne Invasion of Holland by now. Well, I helped a little on that show and got to see it all for the first few days from zero hour. It was quite a sight! We were shooting up flak positions and gun positions and anything else that needed it before the troops came in. There were more planes over there that day than I thought could be in all of England."

Two days later on September 19th, while flying a mission into central Germany, Sim's oxygen supply failed. Because he could not maintain the altitude, he was forced to return to the base in England. Another fighter pilot Lt. Schlack was supposed to escort him back, but due to thick clouds they were separated.

About the time Sim was crossing the German border into Belgium, his plane was hit by small arms fire from the ground, cutting a gas line. His engine began sputtering and then died, so he knew he was being forced to make a dead stick, wheels up crash landing between Mons and Charleroi. When he came down out of the clouds, he spotted an open field where an old farmer was plowing with a team of large horses. He narrowly missed the man and crash-landed in his plowed field. Because Sim had already opened his canopy in preparation for the crash and he was coming in at over 100 miles per hour, he was showered and covered by the freshly plowed dirt. Frantically, he turned off all the switches to prevent a possible fire. In his haste to get out of the plane, he was yanked back by his seat belt and radio cord. He cut the lines and climbed down out of the plane.

By then the farmer had come running up. Unfortunately, he could not speak English. A crowd began gathering. Some men in a Jeep who were dressed partly in German uniforms arrived. They also could not speak English. One of them pointed to Sim's shoulder holster carrying his Colt .45. Even though Sim knew they wanted his pistol, he acted like he did not understand and refused to give it to them. He was actually prepared to shoot them if they tried taking it.

About that time the city treasurer of Charleroi, who happened to also be the local leader of the French Underground, arrived with his daughter. Fortunately, she could speak a little English. Sim learned that the men in partial German uniforms were not really Germans; they were members of the French Underground. They had only wanted his pistol as a souvenir. The leader ordered the others to guard Sim's plane.

Apparently, the nearby school located two blocks away, either saw what had happened or had been notified because they dismissed school in order for the teachers and children to observe the plane. Within a few minutes, students began climbing all over it, and Sim had to warn them through the interpreter to get them off because the .50 caliber machine guns were still armed.

As they stood there attempting to communicate, Sim found one of their customs oddly uncomfortable. If the men needed to urinate, they would simply turn to the side, whip it out right there in public, and relieve themselves. He was a little embarrassed since there were women and young children around.

Relieved, he learned that the Germans had been driven back about seven miles from the location, and he was invited home with the city treasurer for a welcomed warm bath, a glass of wine, and a hot meal. His soft bed was a welcomed relief, except for the too friendly Belgian bedbugs that were also happy for his visit. Had it not been for the hospitality of these people, Sim would not have made it back safely to his base.

On his way back to base, Sim caught a ride with some American M. P.s driving a load of German prisoners to a prison camp. There was no room up front for him, so he had to ride in the back, guarding the prisoners with his Colt .45. One of the German prisoners was an arrogant S. S. officer, a doctor who had refused to treat his own men. When the officer attempted to start an uprising, Sim "cooled him off pretty quickly." When they transferred them to a truck, the officer ordered one of his men to sit on the floor so he could have the seat. Incensed, the M. P.s forced the officer onto the floor.

Eventually, Sim made his way back to base aboard a C-47 Transport plane. When he called his C. O. and reported what had happened, a Jeep was sent to retrieve him. Even though he had only been Missing-In-Action for two days, a telegram had already been sent to Mid and Ida notifying them of the fact. Their world seemed to be crashing in on them. They were not yet sure Mutt would fully recover, and now they had a son who they feared had been killed in action.

Sim would fly a total of 33 missions over Germany before war's end. Although he began flying the P-47 Thunderbolt, he later flew the P-51 Mustang. No matter which plane he flew, he always believed God was his co-pilot. He had spared his life on so many occasions, and he would always remain grateful.

After the war and Sim had flown back to New York, he set his bag down, which included his Colt .45 that he had intended to keep as a souvenir, to make a phone call home to let his parents know he had made it back to the states. When he turned around to pick up his bag, it was missing. Some thief had snatched it from him.

The 361st Officers quarters was an "E" shaped building, this is a view of the center ... (Bomberger)

Aerial View of Martlesham Heath (Richason)

Sim's living quarters
at Martlesham Heath

Fighter base

Murphy and Sim standing
by Sim's P-47 Thunderbolt

Sim standing on wing
of his P-51 Mustang

Service Parade

Quartet of Brothers in Services

Four Houston brothers, one wounded by shrapnel in France and now in a British hospital, are stationed across the world on various fighting fronts. All entered the service voluntarily. They are the sons of Mr. and Mrs. J. M. Higginbotham of 2501 Lone Oak street and the brothers of Mrs. H. F. Sterner of 438 Kress street.

Sgt. Murphy Higginbotham, wounded Ranger, holds the Bronze Star and the Purple Heart. An infantryman for four years, he was based in Ireland and England before landing with Allied forces on D-day. His wife and son, Murphy Daniel, live at 2718 Trenton street.

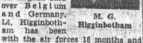

"All I can say now is that God was my constant companion and was responsible for my safe return," wrote First Lt. Merriam G. Higginbotham, 25, P-47 pilot, of a mission from his English base over Belgium and Germany. Lt. Higginbotham has been with the air forces 16 months and overseas since July.

M. G. Higginbotham

Lt. Higginbotham's troubles on the particular mission of which he wrote began when his flight of Thunderbolts moved into some clouds in an effort to gain altitude. Suddenly flak burst through all around them, and when the Houston pilot finally flew his way clear of both clouds and steel, every other plane in his flight had disappeared. With a dead radio, a near-empty gas tank, and only his compass to guide him, the lieutenant was headed for England when he ran into bad weather. The rest of the way home he flew by instruments, reaching his field just as his engine began to sputter. "I just had one hole in my right wing and a lot of scratches and dents from the flack," he reported to his family.

M. J. Higginbotham **M. D. Higginbotham**

The last of the four Higginbothams to enter service and one of the three now overseas is Radioman Third Milton J. Higginbotham, somewhere in the Pacific. A veteran of two years in the Navy, he is 19.

Sgt. Marvin D. Higginbotham, 29, has been in service seven years and is now an air forces ordnanceman. He is based at Barksdale Field, La., since his transfer from his former station, Fort Sam Houston.

Seaman First ...

uston Pres
S, THURSDAY, SEPTEMBER 14, 1944————PAGE SE

Sgt. Murphy Higginbotham, Ranger, Wounded in France

A veteran of the D-day invasion of France, Sgt. Murphy Higginbotham, Ranger, was wounded Aug. 1 and now is convalescing in a hospital in England. His wife lives at 2718 Trenton.

In a letter written in the hospital, the sergeant told Mrs. Higginbotham that the week before he was injured he was hemmed behind a hedgerow with the Germans no more than 50 yards away. Protected by the night, other Americans were able to bring the cornered men supplies and their mail. Once his letters included a picture of his son, Murphy Daniel, whom he has never seen, and he had to wait until dawn to distinguish the baby's features. Finally, though, Sgt. Higginbotham was hit by enemy shrapnel.

This Ranger has been a member of the infantry for four years and has been overseas since October. He was based first in Ireland and then moved to England.

Sgt. Higginbotham has been awarded the Bronze Star Medal for gallantry in action and the Purple Heart. He is the son of Mr. and Mrs. J. M. Higginbotham of 2501 Lone Oak.

* * *

SGT. MURPHY HIGGINBOTHAM

105

13

After the war was over and Mid and Ida's sons returned home, the huge boulder that weighed them down was finally removed. Maybe things would return to somewhat normal. However, Boonie was still drinking and fighting. One evening Mid and Scooter were sitting on the front porch, just enjoying the peace and quiet. Marvin was out in the yard when Boonie came in intoxicated.

When Boonie reached the front steps, mild-mannered Mid began trying to talk some sense into his son. Becoming agitated and increasingly disrespectful, Boonie climbed the steps toward his father. Sensing trouble, Marvin quickly picked up a board. When Boonie lurched toward Mid, Marvin whacked him from behind with the board, knocking him off the porch and breaking his leg.

The next day after Boonie had sobered up and sat nursing his leg, he remarked to Scooter and Marvin, "Damn! Pa's a tough son-of-a-bitch!" No one ever told him it wasn't his dad who had walloped him.

Boonie studied to be a draftsman and was quite an accomplished cartoon artist. He drew a series of cartoons based on bird characters he had observed while in the Navy, his favorite being a pelican. In fact his comic strips had been accepted for publication with the McNaught syndicate, a national and international publisher. However, Boonie did not believe he could keep up with the demands for that much new material every week, so he turned down the contract offer.

He later hired on with the Houston Belt & Terminal Railroad. He began dating a young woman. Sometime later, the family learned that Boonie's girlfriend was carrying his child. The young lady wanted to marry him, but he was not interested in that kind of responsibility, so his son was born in Jacksonville, Texas and adopted by a sweet Christian family who had lost their own baby boy. Over fifty years later, my sister Linda located him through DNA testing. He was given the name Larry Kee.

Boonie last worked as a draftsman for Bernard Johnson, an engineer in Houston. On December 2, 1965, he failed to show up at work. When his boss sent someone to check on him at his house across the street, they found him dead. He was 40 years old.

Marvin began making knives out of scrap metal. These included butcher knives used for processing hogs or kitchen knives used for slicing meat. Although he intended to sell them for a profit, he was so kind-hearted, he wound up giving most of them away to friends and neighbors. He was also the quiet brother who prided himself in settling disputes with the younger ones. Marvin also loved cooking and experimenting with recipes. He gained quite the reputation for his Mulligan Stew. That is where he acquired the nickname "Mully Grub."

As far as the family knew, he never fathered any children. He spent his days at home with his parents seeing to their needs and working in his welding shop making knives and other such items. Years later he would even build a small cannon for Scooter. Marvin died on May 16, 1968 at the age of 53.

Mildred eventually became a well-known real estate broker in Houston. In fact she sold a huge section of land to NASA. Her office was located on Aldine-Bender, in front of her huge mobile home park. Mildred had a reputation for compassion, sometimes to a fault. Whenever a tenant gave her a hard-luck story, she would let them stay without paying rent. She had such a soft heart for people. I actually worked in her real estate office for a short time during my teenage years.

She raised two children, Robert John and Cherilyn. Many years later after her adult son went missing, she established the Missing Person's Bureau in Houston and Galveston. She was instrumental in reuniting several families through her intense efforts. She never found her own son before her death on January 7, 1997. She was 79 years old.

Sim married his sweetheart, Ethyl "Bubbles" Wells. They built their own house, complete with an elaborate machine shop, the Little Crest Machine Shop, next door. They raised four children, Arleen, Alan, and twin girls, Donna and Doris. He made quite a comfortable living for his family and provided many pieces of equipment to the oil industry that was booming after the war. Scooter designed a large cannon and had Sim fabricate it for him. We used it for many years to celebrate Fourth of Julys, New Years', or any other event our family desired. Eventually Sim moved his shop closer into town.

Sim's family became an important part of their church family, as well as ours. They worked with the Helmers Street Baptist Church for many years. As elementary-aged girls, my sister Deborah and I attended several times with them. Because the twins were our age, we spent so much time together during our earlier years. If we weren't at each other's houses or family get-togethers, we were traveling together on camping trips.

My sister Deborah and I were there with Sim's family when he had his second heart bypass surgery. He never survived it; he died at the age of 68 on February 11, 1987.

Mutt and Lucille were blessed over the years with nine children; however, two daughters died. Selma Lucille was born prematurely and died the same day on October 22, 1942. Mildred Ida "Daughty" died of measles and pneumonia on March 15, 1958 at the age of two. She had been treated for the wrong illness, and it was too late for her when they discovered the mistake. This tragedy only hastened her father's downfall. Their other children were: Danny, Marilyn, Karen, Paul, Donald, Melvin, and Jean.

Mutt's addiction to alcohol and tranquilizers had become an overwhelming problem for his family. As long as he was sober, he was a kind person, but when he was intoxicated, he became increasingly abusive to Lucille and his children. Because she truly loved him, she had tried everything she knew to help him overcome his demons, but the war had taken a toll on him. When he threatened to kill Danny, his first-born son who he had seen for the first time while being pinned down in a foxhole in France, Lucille knew she could stay no longer. She loaded up the children and left.

The war had charged many thousands of soldiers a toll, a human toll; sometimes that toll was paid by the emotional instability of those soldiers. Murphy had seen too much: too many obliterated bodies on the beach; too much rotten and

110

stinking flesh; too many encounters with the enemy face-to-face as their lives were finalized; too many lost buddies. It was too much from which to rid his mind.

Even though his doctor knew he was drowning his memories with alcohol, he kept prescribing tranquilizers. The military taught you how to kill, not how to heal. No matter how hard he tried to drown his emotional pain, Mutt could never erase those images from his mind. Alcohol and drugs only led to his own destruction. Perhaps that was exactly what he was trying to do. Perhaps he wondered why, out of so many who had given their lives on the field of battle, he had survived. Perhaps...

Murphy eventually succumbed to his emotional wounds on July 30, 1965 at the age of only 44 years. He was laid to rest beside his two-year-old daughter in the Rosewood Cemetery in Humble, Texas.

We supported Lucille's decision to leave Mutt and often visited them. As teenagers, my youngest sister, Linda, and I traveled with them on several camping trips. One trip was to the new Disney World in Florida. Another was to the beach in Galveston. Others were to Colorado. We still hold those memories close to our hearts.

14

When Scooter was about 12 years old, he decided to join the Woodsdale neighborhood football team. The team was fully suited in uniforms when he began playing with them, and it made him feel close to this group of boys, some who were a little older than he. It was customary for them to play out in a cow pasture nearby. The boys loved their little group and all the camaraderie that came with it. Not only did they love playing the game, it gave them a chance to crack jokes and just put a little fun in their lives.

One day while they were playing, Scooter ran out for a long pass, dove to catch the ball, but slid face-first into a wet, fresh cow patty. The other boys erupted in laughter. Humiliated, poor Scooter ran home to wash up. He was never allowed to live that one down by his other teammates.

In 1948, when Scooter was 14, a new family moved next-door to their east. At that time, John and Effie Pierce had three daughters, Edna, Fay, and Mary Ann "Merdie," as well as two sons, John Jr. and Paul. Later they would bare two more sons, Lewis and Michael "Mike." They lived in their garage apartment until they built their new house; the address was 2509 Lone Oak. After Scooter and Edna began dating a few years later, the Pierce family became close with the Higginbothams.

Scooter had dropped out of high school his freshman year and opted to train at the Flory Telegraph School in order to work for the railroad as a telegrapher. Boonie had encouraged him to go that route, and he promised to help him get a job at the Houston Belt & Terminal where he was employed. After he completed his course on December 14, 1950, he was immediately hired by the Santa Fe Railroad in Galveston. Then he was transferred to Alvin for a short time before being sent to Bellville. Because he was tired of being shipped to different locations far from home, he applied for a job with the Houston Belt & Terminal. They were anxious to hire him; he was told he was the youngest telegrapher on the Belt. Bringing home an adequate steady salary allowed him to purchase a house on July Street, a couple of miles from his parents. He also bought his first car, a 1948 Frazier. He was 17 years old.

He and 15 year-old Edna began dating in February 1952. Impressed by his maturity and the fact that he already owned his own house and car, it was easy for her to say yes when he got the nerve to ask her out. They began dating, and it wasn't long before they fell head-over-heals in love with each other.

On December 13 of that year, they were united in matrimony. Since Edna attended church with Louie Welch, who preached occasionally at North Houston Church of Christ, he performed the small ceremony for them at his home. At that time he also served on the Houston City Council. Twelve years later Louis Welch would be elected mayor of Houston.

The next December 23, I was born. Because it was unusually cold in the house on July Street, they brought me home to her parents' garage apartment. Mom was so sick, my grandmother Pierce actually helped breastfeed me a few times. Mom's youngest brother Mike was only 10 months old, so "Mother" volunteered to help. [*Mike actually became more of a brother than an uncle because we grew up together. In fact he lived with us on and off after his father died. Because he had dropped out of school in seventh grade, I wanted him to experience some of what he had missed in high school, so I invited him to my junior and senior proms.*]

We lived there until Mom and Dad bought a quarter acre from Grandma and Grandpa Higginbotham and built a house on the west side, next door to them. The next December 16, 1954, my sister Deborah was born. We were considered "Irish Twins" because we were less than one year apart. Four years later my youngest sister Linda was born. It wasn't until my senior year in high school that Mom and Dad were finally blessed with a son, Robert.

Living that close to two sets of parents became uncomfortable for the young couple who were anxious to gain their independence, so they sold and moved to a neighborhood a few miles distance, but we grew up with so many great memories of the two houses on Lone Oak. It was the place where both families gathered.

If we were visiting with Dad's family, we would often walk around the fence that separated the two houses and go visit Mom's family before leaving for home. It was a unique situation and one that I fondly recall from time to time. It was truly "the girl next-door" kind of thing.

Dad worked for the Belt his entire career, a total of 31 years, until he was hit one day by a train in the railyard while it was backing up on the new ribbon rail. The ribbon rail was quieter than the traditional rail. You did not hear the clickety-clack you would hear on the previous style. Because Dad had a hearing loss in one ear, and he was walking between two sets of tracks, he would occasionally look behind him to make sure there were no trains coming. He simply missed the one that hit him.

Thankfully, he survived, but that accident broke two bones in his back and bruised him profusely, ending his career and sending him into an early disability retirement. In later years, he developed nephritis and had to eventually go on dialysis. Becoming weaker over the years, he fell one morning and hit his head on the floor. Mom had him rushed to the hospital. When we went to see him, he still had not lost his sense of humor. He knew he had left blood on the kitchen floor where he had fallen, so he told us Ashley, their schnauzer, could lick it up. Later that night he passed away from a brain hemorrhage.

Considering all things, Mid and Ida had left quite a legacy. They had borne seven children and had lived to see 18 of their 20 grandchildren. One of my last memories of Grandma before her passing was when she came to visit me at Hermann Hospital in Houston. Because I was born without an artery to my left kidney, I had become critically ill at the age of 12 and had been on complete bed rest for three months prior to my surgery to remove the dead one. Even though I was still under anesthesia and I couldn't really see her, I remember hearing her sweet voice of concern and her speaking to me. That was in July 1967. Early in September she was rushed to St. Joseph Hospital where she suffered from one heart attack after another. This was shortly before heart bypass surgery was an option. Dad visited her and told her how wonderful of a mother she had been and let her know how much she was truly loved by her family. My earnest hope is that she fully understood that. She died on September 14th, two months after visiting me in the hospital.

Grandpa was a lost soul after that and pined away until his death the following July 19th. I remember him visiting our house in Porter after Grandma's passing, but his eyes and spirit were greatly diminished. The love of his life was gone forever, and he just wanted to be with her again. He was laid to rest beside her in the Brookside Memorial Cemetery in Houston. They had both fought the good fight; now they rested in the arms of their Lord.

I often reflect on the days of my childhood and how much my grandparents meant to me. Although times were hard for them most of their lives due to the lack of air-conditioning, washing machines, and just basic household appliances we take for granted now, times were simpler. Families appreciated one another more because they spent more days together visiting, reminiscing, and making new memories. Time seemed to pass slower then. Maybe it was my youth and innocence. Thanks to our grandparents and parents who had laid a concrete foundation for us, we children were living our dreams and creating solid foundations for our own future families without understanding how quickly time would fly. When I married Gary Nichols in 1973, I took on his last name, but that Higginbotham blood still runs through my heart and my veins.

Grandma and Grandpa never owned an air-conditioner or a modern washing machine, but they were able to listen to news reports over the radio and eventually watch a black and white television. Thankfully, they *did* learn through those reports about women gaining the right to vote. They *did* witness the gradual transition from the horse and buggy days to the use of automobiles and air planes. They *did* witness our nation pulling together as **one** to rebuild our nation after both

World Wars. They *did* witness and were part of that national pride and effort. Unfortunately, they *did* learn about President Kennedy's assassination. They *did* witness Martin Luther King Jr.'s nonviolent efforts to gain the rights of black people to enjoy the same liberties as others. They *did* participate in their local church functions and were faithful Christians who believed in loving their neighbors and helping them as they did themselves. They did not depend on a government tit to sustain them; they depended on God, themselves and one another. They embodied the heart and soul of America's heartland.

Sadly, my grandparents did *not* live to see man land on the moon or the computer age greatly improve our nation's workforce. Thankfully, they did *not* live to witness our nation being infiltrated over the last few decades by Socialist activists and anarchists who had promised during my early childhood to divide and conquer our nation from within. They did *not* see many of our nation's young people being brainwashed through our colleges, universities, and media. Thank God they did *not* have to face the pandemic of 2020! They had been through enough.

I hope and pray our current generations clean house and come together once again like our forefathers did. Through their hard work, determination, and God's blessings, they helped make this the greatest nation on earth. If we all have that same work ethic, determination, *faith* in our creator *and hope* in our hearts, we can do it again and hopefully pass on that spirit to those who follow.

Scooter & Edna with Louis Welch

Wedding Day December 13, 1952

Mid and Ida holding Vivian

1954

Epilogue

With the passing of Grandma and Grandpa Higginbotham, their home was turned over to Mildred, who put it on the market. George Foreman, the Heavy Weight Boxing Champion, purchased their property. He tore the old house down and built a church on their site. He was a great neighbor to my other grandmother Effie Pierce, who was still living next door.

Since my grandfather Pierce had already passed years earlier, George was kind enough to mow her yard. "Mother" would always yell out and remind him not to cut her small pecan trees down. I'm quite sure that was a comical sight. When Mother died in 1987, George also bought her property because he wanted to build a daycare beside the church.

Because I wanted to preserve the memories I had of the two homes, I was reluctant to drive by and see the changes. Decades later I finally did. The places were just not the same. It would not have mattered to me if George had built a mansion. I would have preferred the two houses on Lone Oak.